D1425951

STUDENT UNIT GUIDE

NEW EDITION

CCEA AS Biology Unit 2
Organisms and Biodiversity

John Campton

PHILIP ALLAN

Philip Allan, an imprint of Hodder Education, an Hachette UK company, Market Place, Deddington, Oxfordshire OX15 0SE

Orders
Bookpoint Ltd, 130 Milton Park, Abingdon, Oxfordshire, OX14 4SB
tel: 01235 827827
fax: 01235 400401
e-mail: education@bookpoint.co.uk
Lines are open 9.00 a.m.–5.00 p.m., Monday to Saturday, with a 24-hour message answering service.
You can also order through the Philip Allan website: www.philipallan.co.uk

Cover photo: Fotolia

Typeset by Integra Software Services Pvt. Ltd., Pondicherry, India

Printed in Dubai

Hachette UK's policy is to use papers that are natural, renewable and recyclable products and made from wood grown in sustainable forests. The logging and manufacturing processes are expected to conform to the environmental regulations of the country of origin.

P02117

Contents

Getting the most from this book

Questions & Answers

Question 3

Question 3

Sand dunes may differ in their species composition. The diagram below is a vertical section through one particular sand dune system.

Describe how you would sample the area depicted in the diagram and use the results to illustrate quantitatively the zonation of the vegetation.

(6 marks)

Total: 6 marks

ⓔ This question assesses AO3 — understanding of biology as an experimental science. In this case, you are asked about how you would undertake an ecological study of an area where there is obvious zonation. Notice that 6 marks are available, so a detailed answer is required.

Student A
Set a line transect through the dunes ✓ and place quadrats ✓ along this at 5 metre intervals ✓. Calculate the total percentage cover of all the plants in the quadrat ✗. Then put the results in a table and compare the different percentage covers of different zones within the sand dunes ✗.

ⓔ 3/6 marks awarded There are only three correct points given here. It is not sufficient to determine the total percentage cover of all plants — the determination must be for each species. No attempt is made to suggest how the zonation would be illustrated — for example by a series of kite diagrams (one for each species) with percentage cover (y-axis) plotted against position along the sand dunes.

Student B
You would start at the embryo dunes and randomly sample ✓ the area using quadrats ✓. You would determine the percentage cover ✓ of each plant species. You would then move to the next area and continue ✓ until the landward area is reached. You would record the results.

ⓔ 4/6 marks awarded Student B has provided the basis of a sampling procedure: random sampling; sampling at sites transecting the dunes; use of quadrats; determination of percentage cover to measure abundance. However, there is no reference to the

Unit 2: Organisms and Biodiversity

69

About this book

The aim of this book is to help you prepare for the AS Unit 2 examination for CCEA biology. It also offers support to students studying A2 biology, since topics at A2 rely on an understanding of AS material.

The **Content Guidance** section covers the specification content of AS Unit 2. It should be used as a study aid as you meet each topic, when you prepare for end-of-topic tests and during your final revision. For each of the seven topics there are Examiner tips and Knowledge checks in the margin. Answers to the Knowledge checks are provided at the end of the book. At the end of each topic there is a list of the practical work with which you are expected to be familiar. This is followed by a comprehensive yet succinct summary of the points covered in each topic.

The **Questions and Answers** section provides two exemplar papers for you to try. There are answers written by two students together with examiner's comments on their performances and how they might have been improved. These will be particularly useful during your final revision. There is a range of question styles that you will encounter in the AS Unit 2 exam, and the students' answers and examiner's comments should help with your examination technique.

Developing your understanding

It is important that through your AS course you develop effective study techniques.

- You must *not* simply read through the content of this book.
- Your understanding will be better if you are *active* in your learning. You could take the information given in this book and present it in different ways. Using the blood transport system in a mammal as an example you could do the following:
  - a series of bullet points summarising the key points
  - an annotated diagram of the heart to show its structure with labelled features and brief notes of function
  - an annotated graph to show pressure changes during a cardiac cycle with notes explaining the phases and points at which valves are opened and closed
  - a spider diagram of the heart to include reference to its structure, the wave of excitation, the phases of the cardiac cycle, pressure changes and the operation of valves
- Compile a glossary of terms for each topic. Key terms are shown in **bold** (with a few in the margin). For each, you should be able to provide a definition. This will develop your understanding of the language used in biology and help you when quality of written communication is assessed.
- Write essays on different topics. For example, an essay on transport in plants will test your understanding of the entire topic and give you practice for the Section B question.
- *Think* about the information in this book so that you can *apply* your understanding in unfamiliar situations. Ultimately you should be able to deal with questions that set a topic in a new context.
- Ensure that you are familiar with the practical skills expected in this unit so that you can answer questions on *'How science works'*.

- Use past questions and other exercises to develop all the skills that examiners must test.
- Use the topic summaries to check that you have covered all the material you need to know and also as a brief survey of each topic.

The AS Unit 2 paper

The AS Unit 2 examination lasts 1 hour 30 minutes and is worth 75 marks. There are two sections. In Section A all the questions are structured though there is a variety of question styles. In Section B there is a single question, which may be presented in several parts, and which should be answered in continuous prose.

Be aware that the examiners must test a range of skills. These are called assessment objectives and are described in the CCEA specification. At AS, examiners must design the paper to show the following balance of marks:

Assessment Objective	Description	Marks
AO1	Knowledge and understanding	32
AO2	Application of knowledge and understanding	32
AO3	*How Science Works*	11

Questions towards the start of the paper and initial sub-parts of questions tend to assess straightforward 'knowledge and understanding' (AO1). There will also be questions that present information in new contexts and may test your skills in analysing and evaluating data (AO2).

AO3 may be assessed by questions that ask you to evaluate experimental work. You may also be asked to demonstrate graphical or drawing skills, or to organise raw data into a table.

You are expected to use good English and accurate scientific terminology in all your answers. Quality of written communication is assessed throughout the paper and is specifically awarded a maximum of 2 marks in Section B.

Examiner tip
The CCEA biology specification is available from www.ccea.org.uk. You will also be able to access past papers and mark schemes.

Content Guidance

Principles of exchange and transport

Living cells require certain substances to maintain their metabolic processes. These substances include:

- oxygen for aerobic respiration
- glucose and fatty acids as substrates for respiratory metabolism
- fatty acids for the synthesis of phospholipids required for the production of membranes
- amino acids for the synthesis of proteins (e.g. enzymes)
- ions to maintain water potential, as enzyme cofactors and for other aspects of metabolism (e.g. in plant cells, nitrate ions to provide nitrogen for amino acid synthesis and phosphate for the synthesis of phospholipids)
- water as a solvent

These substances are either synthesised within the cell (in which case other substances are usually required), or released from storage molecules within the organism (and perhaps transported through the organism), or obtained from the environment.

All living cells need to remove the toxic by-products of their metabolic processes. These include:

- carbon dioxide from aerobic respiration (in animal cells and microorganisms, and from plant cells not actively carrying out photosynthesis)
- oxygen from photosynthesis (in green plant cells)
- urea and ammonia from excess amino acids (in animals, since plants generally only synthesise the amino acids they require)

To summarise, animal tissues need to obtain:

- oxygen from the air (or from water if they are aquatic)
- glucose, fatty acids and amino acids from food
- water

Carbon dioxide and nitrogenous waste have to be removed from animal tissues.

The tissues of flowering plants need:

- oxygen from the air, especially at night
- carbon dioxide from the air during the day
- inorganic ions (which, together with sugars from photosynthesis, produce amino acids etc.) from the soil solution
- water from the soil solution

Depending on the time of day, either carbon dioxide or oxygen is removed from plant tissues.

Examiner tip
Be careful about the use of terms here. An **absorptive surface** allows the uptake of soluble substances — for example, the absorption of products of digestion in the ileum or of water and ions by root hairs. A **gas exchange surface** allows oxygen to move through in one direction and carbon dioxide in the opposite direction. It is sometimes referred to as a **respiratory surface** because the respiratory gases, oxygen and carbon dioxide, are involved.

Knowledge check 1

What inorganic ion do plants need to absorb in order to make amino acids?

Thus, organisms need to absorb or exchange substances with their environment and transport these substances within the organism.

The exchange of substances

There are a number of factors that influence the absorption or exchange of substances.

The exchange of substances occurs only at **moist permeable surfaces**. Aquatic organisms, organisms that live in the soil and even some terrestrial organisms, such as amphibians, all have moist and so permeable body surfaces. This is not the case with terrestrial organisms such as mammals and flowering plants. To prevent water loss by evaporation, mammals possess an impermeable surface (skin with a cornified layer onto which an oily substance is secreted) while the aerial parts of flowering plants are covered in a waxy cuticle secreted by the epidermis. This means that mammals and flowering plants must have specialised absorptive or exchange surfaces.

The need for specialised absorptive or exchange surfaces depends on the size and shape of the organism because both these factors affect an organism's **surface area-to-volume ratio**. The surface area is represented by the total number of cells in direct contact with the surrounding environment. The volume is the total three-dimensional space occupied by metabolically active tissues. The absorptive surface area is a measure of the rate of supply of metabolites to tissues. The volume of the organism is a measure of its demand for metabolites. An organism must be capable of taking up sufficient material to satisfy its needs. Therefore, the surface area-to-volume ratio is critical — it must be sufficiently large.

The influence of size on the surface area-to-volume ratio is shown graphically in Figure 1, in which cubes of different dimensions are used as the example.

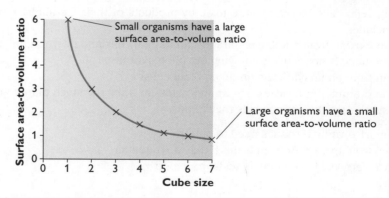

Figure 1 The relationship between size and surface area-to-volume ratio

While this relationship has been calculated for cubes, the principle is true for all regular shapes. *Small* organisms have a *large* surface area-to-volume ratio. The external surface of a small organism can be used as a gas exchange surface because the large surface area is able to supply sufficient oxygen to the small volume. For example, an earthworm is small enough for its body surface to be used for gas exchange.

A larger organism has a small surface area compared with its large volume, i.e. a small surface area-to-volume ratio. The large volume creates a demand for oxygen

Gas exchange is the process by which oxygen reaches cells and carbon dioxide is removed from them. It should not be confused with respiration. **Respiration** is the release of energy from food to synthesise ATP within all living cells.

Knowledge check 2

Calculate the surface area-to-volume ratio of a cuboid body of dimension 1 × 2 × 3.

which the small surface area is unable to supply. Therefore, large organisms need specialised permeable surfaces whereby the absorption or exchange area is increased to satisfy the needs of the organism.

The rate at which an organism requires substances depends on its metabolic rate. An organism with a high metabolic rate has a high oxygen requirement and, therefore, possesses specialised, large, gas exchange surfaces. This can be illustrated by comparing the mouse and the frog, which are organisms of similar size. The mouse has a metabolic rate and oxygen consumption approximately ten times greater than that of a frog, and has a proportionately bigger gas exchange surface. The frog's lungs are simple sacs, while the mouse has spongy lungs consisting of millions of microscopic alveoli. The large surface area is essential for the high rate of oxygen uptake required for the high metabolic rate of the mouse.

To summarise, an organism requires a specialised absorptive surface if it is terrestrial (with an impermeable surface), large (with a small surface area-to-volume ratio) or has a high metabolic rate. Methods of increasing the area of an absorptive surface include:
- evagination (outfolding) of the surface
- invagination (infolding) of the surface
- flattening of the organism

Organisms with a flattened shape have a large surface area-to-volume ratio. A cube of $1 \times 1 \times 1$ arbitrary units has a surface area-to-volume ratio of 6. If this cube is flattened to dimensions of $0.1 \times 10 \times 1$ arbitrary units, it has the same volume but the surface area-to-volume ratio is 22.2, an increase of nearly four-fold. Flattening not only increases the surface area-to-volume ratio, it also decreases the distance over which substances have to be moved.

Skills development: numeracy skills — calculations

To gain a better understanding, you should go over the calculation of surface area-to-volume ratios shown in Figure 1 and described above. Remember that the examination will require you to carry out at least one calculation, so practice is a good idea. The ratio is calculated as the proportion of one value to another. Apart from ratio, you might also be asked to calculate magnification (see Student Unit Guide AS Unit 1), percentage, percentage change and rate.

Percentage means out of 100. It is calculated by dividing a value by the total and multiplying by 100. Percentages are calculated in J-tube analysis (determination of the percentage O_2 and percentage CO_2 content of air samples).

To calculate a percentage change, divide the difference (final value subtracted from the initial value) by the initial amount and multiply by 100. You should be aware that:
- a negative change represents a decrease
- a positive change means that there is an increase
- a 100% increase equates to a doubling in the quantity
- a 1000% increase is a ten-fold increase

The rate of a process is calculated as the change per unit time.

Examiner tip

Never say that small organisms have a large surface area — the surface area of a small organism is small! It is the surface area-to-volume ratio that is large.

Knowledge check 3

Give three reasons why humans need a specialised gas exchange surface (i.e. lungs).

Table 1 shows some important examples of efficient absorptive surfaces in flowering plants and mammals.

Table 1 Absorptive surfaces in flowering plants and mammals

Absorptive surface	Structure	Function
Leaf mesophyll	The leaf is a flattened structure (its thinness ensures a short diffusion distance) with a tightly packed upper palisade mesophyll layer and a loosely packed lower spongy mesophyll layer	Wide expanse of palisade tissue is efficient at trapping light; the loose arrangement of the spongy layer provides an air space system through the leaf and creates a huge surface for gas exchange
Root hairs	Tubular extensions of the epidermal cells of the young root	Increase greatly the surface area of the root for the uptake of oxygen, water and ions
Alveoli	Small (diameter 0.2 mm) sacs, occurring in clusters and in vast numbers within the mammalian lung; in human lungs there are 700 million, providing a total surface area of 70 m^2	Huge, moist surface area provides for efficient gas exchange; the alveolar walls are thin (0.1–1.0 µm), so the diffusion distance is short
Capillaries	Small (diameter 5–10 µm), thin-walled blood vessels, with a total length of 100 000 km and surface area of 1000 m^2 in the human body	Extensive networks throughout the body represent a huge surface area for the exchange of molecules between the blood and the body tissues; the number and distribution of capillaries is such that no cell is further away than 50 µm from a capillary, i.e. the diffusion distance is minute

Absorptive surface	Structure	Function
Erythrocytes (red blood cells) Top view Side view	Small (diameter 8 µm) flexible biconcave discs, flattened and depressed in the centre, with a dumbbell-shaped cross section	The biconcave disc shape greatly increases the surface area-to-volume ratio for efficient uptake of oxygen; the thinness of the cell, particularly where it is depressed in the centre, allows oxygen to diffuse to all the haemoglobin packed into the cell

Knowledge check 4

What two features of erythrocytes provide them with a large surface area-to-volume ratio?

The transport of substances

The molecules in gases and liquids move constantly and at random. If there is a difference in the concentration of molecules within an area, a net movement of the molecules occurs, resulting in the molecules becoming evenly distributed. This is illustrated in Figure 2.

Examiner tip

Questions often begin by asking for the definition of a term. As a part of your revision, construct a list of definitions for all the terms shown in bold in this chapter. You should also complete a similar exercise for each of the following chapters.

Direction of diffusion

Figure 2 Random movement of molecules causes them to become dispersed from an area of high concentration (a) until they are evenly distributed (b)

Such movements are known as **diffusion**. Diffusion can take place across surfaces as long as these are moist, and permeable to the substances.

Diffusion is a sufficiently effective mechanism for the movement of substances across thin surfaces and within thin organisms. For example, a flatworm (an animal with a simple body plan, small, tapering and flattened — about 2 cm long and 2 mm thick) absorbs oxygen at its moist body surface and this oxygen diffuses to all body tissues since these are within easy reach of the surface. However, diffusion alone does not suffice for the movement of substances within large organisms.

Transport of substances in larger organisms occurs by mass flow (Figure 3). In mass flow, unlike diffusion, all the molecules are swept along in the same direction.

Knowledge check 5

How are gases moved across exchange surfaces?

High pressure ⟶ Low pressure

Figure 3 The mass flow of molecules

Knowledge check 6

List the features of a good transport system.

Mass flow is brought about by a pressure difference. Mass flow systems include the xylem and phloem systems of flowering plants and the breathing (ventilation) and blood circulatory systems of mammals. Different mass flow systems have different means of generating a pressure difference (Table 2).

Table 2 Examples of mass flow systems in flowering plants and mammals

Mass flow system	Method of generating a pressure difference	Function of the mass flow system
Xylem system	Tension (negative pressure) in the leaf xylem generated by the transpirational loss of water from the leaves	One-way transport of water and ions from roots to leaves in a flowering plant
Phloem system	Movement is driven by energy from the plant	Two-way flow of organic solutes (e.g. sucrose) in a flowering plant
Breathing (ventilation) system	Pressures in the thorax are alternately decreased (inducing inhalation) and increased (inducing exhalation)	Ventilation of the mammalian lungs, whereby air is alternately drawn in and forced out
Blood circulatory system	High pressure is generated by the muscular heart	Circulation of blood carrying oxygen, glucose, amino acids, fats, carbon dioxide, urea and other substances in a mammal

Knowledge check 7

Explain how thinness helps gaseous exchange *and* means that a transport system is not necessary.

There is an overlap between the principles of exchange and of transport. The flatness of an organism (or of a cell) increases its surface area-to-volume ratio and, therefore, its effectiveness in absorption. However, it also decreases the diffusion path, which is probably more important. An earthworm, though bigger than a flatworm, has a sufficiently large surface area-to-volume ratio to satisfy its gas exchange requirements, but needs an internal transport (blood circulatory) system, since the diffusion distance is too great. A flatworm has no need for an internal transport system, not only because it is thin, but also because its digestive system branches throughout its body so that food is absorbed in close proximity to all tissues (see Figure 4).

Examiner tip

Note that reference has been made to flatworms, earthworms and even frogs, none of which is specified in the content of the unit. This is because you are required not only to have knowledge of the principles of exchange and transport, but to be able to apply your understanding in unfamiliar situations. Therefore, it is better to learn these principles through appropriate examples.

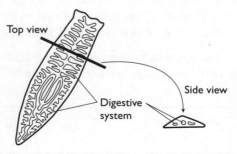

Figure 4 The flatworm: an animal with no need for a blood circulatory system

Summary

- An organism needs to absorb and/or exchange substances with the environment and these substances have to be distributed within the organism.
- Animal tissues require oxygen, the products of digestion and water. Carbon dioxide is released.
- The tissues of flowering plants require oxygen (especially at night), carbon dioxide (during the day), inorganic ions and water.
- Absorption or exchange of substances occurs at moist permeable surfaces.
- A small (aquatic) organism has a large surface area-to-volume ratio, so can supply sufficient oxygen via its surface to satisfy the metabolic demands of its body (volume).
- An organism requires a specialised absorptive/exchange surface if it is terrestrial (with an impermeable surface), if it is large (with a small surface area-to-volume ratio) or if it has a high metabolic rate.
- Specialised absorptive surfaces often involve outfoldings or infoldings, which increase surface area without increasing volume.
- Thinness also increases the surface area-to-volume ratio and, in addition, reduces the diffusion path of substances.
- A transport system is required in larger animals and plants to distribute substances from one site to another.
- Transport systems involve mass flow, the bulk movement of substances due to differences in pressure and a means of generating a pressure difference (often a pump).

Gas exchange in flowering plants and mammals

The biological processes of respiration and photosynthesis require one gas which they exchange for another. The surface over which gas exchange takes place must be:
- permeable to oxygen and carbon dioxide
- moist, since gases must dissolve in water before diffusing into tissue cells

Gas exchange across an exchange surface relies on diffusion. The rate of diffusion across this surface is influenced by a number of factors as defined by Fick's law:

$$\text{rate of diffusion} \propto \frac{\text{surface area} \times \text{difference in concentration}}{\text{length of diffusion pathway}}$$

Fick's law shows that gas exchange is increased:
- if the exchange surface has a large surface area
- if there is a big difference in the concentration of gases on each side of the surface
- if the exchange surface is thin with a short diffusion distance

The higher the metabolic rate of the organism, the greater the need for these principles to be met.

Gas exchange in flowering plants

There are two processes in flowering plants that involve gas exchange: **respiration** and **photosynthesis**. Respiration takes place in all tissues, all the time. Photosynthesis takes place only in green tissues (i.e. those containing chlorophyll), and only during

Examiner tip

In Fick's law, the barrier to diffusion is often referred to as a membrane. The term membrane includes both the cell-surface membrane and the epithelium membrane, i.e. the layer of cells covering an organ.

the daylight hours. Indeed, the rate of photosynthesis depends on the light intensity. So, the maximum rate of photosynthesis occurs when the light intensity is highest, such as at midday. At this point, the rate of photosynthesis greatly exceeds the rate of respiration and so there is a net production of oxygen. At a specific low light intensity (during dawn and dusk) the rate of photosynthesis equals the rate of respiration and so the net exchange of oxygen is zero. This is known as the **compensation point**, since the rate of oxygen production (in photosynthesis) is balanced by the rate of oxygen consumption (in respiration).

These changes in oxygen use and release by a flowering plant are shown in Figure 5.

Figure 5 Changes in oxygen used and released by a plant over a 24-hour period

Respiratory gas exchange in flowering plants

The roots of plants use energy in processes such as cell division (growth) and the active transport of ions from the soil solution. In the growth region, the epidermal cells possess **root hairs**, which increase the surface area-to-volume ratio. In soil that is not waterlogged, root hairs are surrounded by air spaces between the particles of soil. Diffusion of respiratory gases occurs through the cell wall and cell membrane of these root hairs (Figure 6).

Figure 6 Gas exchange in a root hair cell

In stems, especially those of woody plants, the most active cells are those under the surface. Although the stem's outer covering is waterproofed to reduce water loss to the air (and so is impermeable to gases) there are small pores to allow oxygen in and carbon dioxide out.

Plants lack specialised respiratory surfaces and yet can be very large. This is because they lack tissues with a high energy demand and so have low respiration rates.

Photosynthetic gas exchange in flowering plants

The **leaf** is the major photosynthetic organ in a flowering plant. The leaf needs a specialised gas exchange surface because:
- a high rate of photosynthesis is generated
- the concentration of carbon dioxide in the air is low (390 parts per million or 0.039%)

The leaf epidermis, particularly the lower epidermis, possesses **guard cells** that control the opening and closure of **stomata**. The stomata open during the hours of daylight. When open, air, containing carbon dioxide, diffuses into and out of the leaf mesophyll. The carbon dioxide diffuses through an **air space system** provided by the **spongy mesophyll**. Having diffused through the air space system, the carbon dioxide is absorbed by the mesophyll cells (in which the carbon dioxide concentration is low as it is used in photosynthesis). It is this moist mesophyll surface that represents the gas exchange surface (see Figure 7). Since the leaf is *broad and thin*, there is a large surface area and the diffusion distance for gases is short.

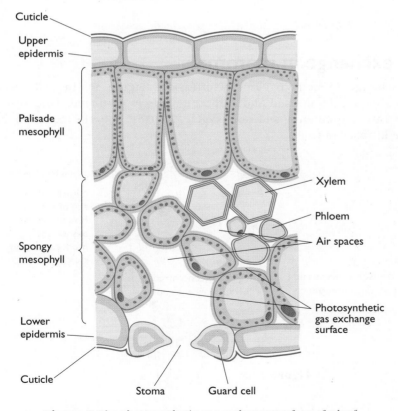

Figure 7 The photosynthetic gas exchange surface of a leaf

Knowledge check 8

Give a reason for plants having a lower metabolic rate than animals.

Knowledge check 9

List three features of leaves that facilitate gas exchange.

Oxygen produced in photosynthesis diffuses out of the cells into the air space and then out through the open stomata. Some oxygen is, of course, used up in respiration.

Plants living in water: hydrophytes

There is much less oxygen dissolved in water than there is oxygen in air, so the stems and leaves of aquatic flowering plants (hydrophytes) have adaptations to facilitate the uptake and movement of oxygen and carbon dioxide (see Figure 8).

Knowledge check 10

Why do floating water plants only have stomata on the upper surface of their leaves?

Figure 8 Adaptations of a hydrophyte (a) stem and (b) leaf

Gas exchange in mammals

Gas exchange in cells occurs by diffusion (Figure 9). In cells respiring aerobically, oxygen is used and carbon dioxide is produced. This affects the concentration gradients and so oxygen diffuses into the cell and carbon dioxide diffuses out.

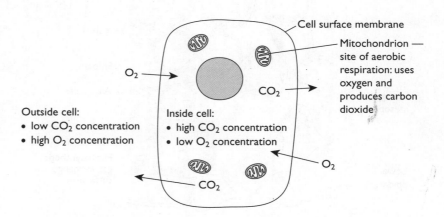

Figure 9 Gas exchange in a respiring cell

The movement of oxygen to cells, and of carbon dioxide out, involves four stages:

- diffusion of gases between respiring cells and the blood
- transport of gases in the blood
- diffusion of gases across the gas exchange surface between the alveolar air and the blood
- ventilation of the lungs with fresh air

Gas exchange in the lungs takes place at the alveolar surface and is particularly efficient. The walls of the alveoli provide a large surface area and consist of thin cells (as do the capillary walls). Concentration gradients are maintained by the ventilation of the lungs and the circulation of blood.

The structure of the lungs

Air is breathed through the nostrils or mouth, and enters or leaves the lungs via the **trachea**. The lungs are situated within the **thorax** (also known as the **thoracic cavity**). The trachea branches into two **bronchi** (singular **bronchus**) which further branch into a series of ever-finer **bronchioles** forming a **bronchial tree**. Each **terminal bronchiole** leads to a cluster of **alveoli**, an **alveolar duct** connecting with each **alveolus**. Each individual alveolus is tightly wrapped in blood capillaries and it is here that gas exchange takes place. The structure of the lung system is shown in Figure 10 (p. 18).

Ventilation of the lungs

Changing the volume of the thoracic cavity changes the air pressure inside the lungs. Air moves from a region of high pressure to a region of low pressure. When the volume of the thorax is increased, the pressure in the lungs is decreased, becoming lower than atmospheric pressure so that air moves into the lungs (inhalation or inspiration). When the volume of the thorax is decreased, the pressure in the lungs is increased, becoming higher than atmospheric pressure so that air moves out of the lungs (exhalation or expiration). The mechanisms of **inhalation** and **exhalation**, during normal breathing, are summarised in Figure 11 (p. 19).

During forced exhalation, such as during hard exercise and coughing, the volume of the thoracic cavity is further reduced by the contraction of the internal intercostal muscles depressing the rib cage.

Alveolar structure and gas exchange

In each human lung there are about 350 million alveoli, each of which is about 200 μm in diameter. Their total surface area is about 70 m^2. Each alveolus is lined with a single layer of squamous epithelial cells only 0.05 μm to 0.3 μm thick. The inner surface of each alveolus is moist. Around each alveolus is a network of blood capillaries so narrow (7–10 μm) that, in order to squeeze through, erythrocytes (red blood cells) are flattened against the capillary walls. These capillaries also have walls one cell thick and consisting of a squamous (also called pavement) epithelium (0.04–0.2 μm thick).

Be careful about the use of terms. **Respiration** occurs in cells and is the release of energy from food to make ATP. **Breathing** refers to the movements of the ribs and diaphragm that cause air to enter and leave (ventilate) the lungs.

Gases can diffuse across the moist, permeable walls of the alveoli. Diffusion of gases between the alveoli and the blood is rapid because:

- concentration gradients are maintained by the ventilation of the lungs and the blood flow through the pulmonary capillaries
- the alveoli and pulmonary capillaries have very large surface areas
- the walls of both alveoli and capillaries are thin and therefore the distance over which diffusion takes place is very short — in fact the distance between alveolar air and the erythrocytes averages only about 0.5 μm.

Knowledge check 11

Explain the advantage of ventilating the lungs.

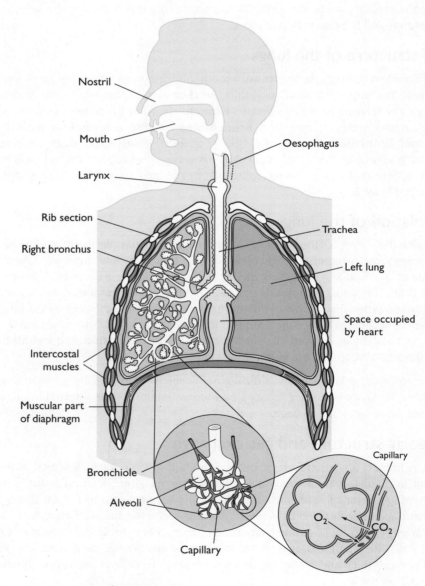

Figure 10 The structure of the lung system

Examiner tip

The alveoli of the lungs exhibit all the features of an efficient gas exchange surface: permeable; moist; large surface area; thin walls; close to transport systems.

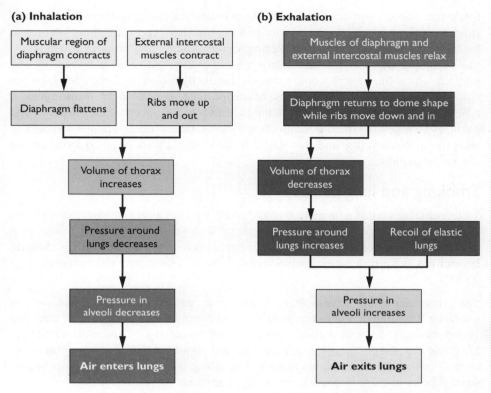

Figure 11 The mechanism of (a) inhalation and (b) exhalation

The structure of an alveolus and associated capillaries is shown in Figure 12 (though the walls, for clarity, have been drawn disproportionately thick).

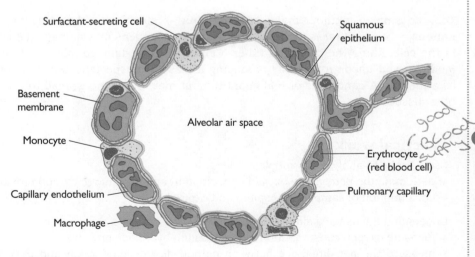

Figure 12 The structure of an alveolus and associated pulmonary capillaries

Since the alveolar surface is situated deep inside the body, evaporation of water from its moist surface is reduced to a minimum. Other types of cell are present in the alveolar wall. **Surfactant-secreting cells** (septal cells) produce a detergent-like substance that reduces the surface tension in the fluid coating the alveoli, and without which the alveoli would collapse due to the cohesive forces between the water molecules lining the air sacs. **Macrophages** (derived from **monocytes**, a type of white blood cell) protect the lungs from a broad spectrum of microbes and particles by ingesting them through phagocytosis. Elastic fibres are also associated with the alveolar walls, and the elastic recoil of the alveoli helps to force air out during exhalation.

Smoking and lung disease

Tobacco smoke contains thousands of toxic substances, many of which are collectively known as tar. Therefore, it is not surprising that smoking has been linked to a number of lung diseases. It is common for smokers to get a combination of **chronic bronchitis** and **emphysema**, which is called chronic obstructive pulmonary disease (COPD).

Tar brings about an inflammatory response in which the airways narrow and excessive amounts of mucus are produced. Furthermore, tar paralyses the cilia that sweep mucus and bacteria away from the lungs, so pathogens and mucus build up. This leads to phlegm production, coughing and breathlessness — the symptoms of chronic bronchitis. The inability to clear mucus and bacteria results in an increased susceptibility to chest infections, including pneumonia.

In emphysema, the inflammatory response to smoke inhalation leads to the breakdown of the walls of the alveoli. This reduces the area available for gas exchange so it becomes difficult to get enough oxygen. There is also a loss of elastic fibres in the alveolar walls. Therefore, exhalation becomes more difficult because the ability of the alveoli to recoil following inhalation is reduced.

Tobacco smoke contains many **carcinogens** — substances that may induce **cancer** — of which tar is the most important. Carcinogens may damage the DNA in the cells lining the bronchial tubes. Cells with DNA damage may divide in a modified and uncontrolled way producing a mass of unspecialised cells known as a tumour. A cancerous or malignant tumour may, over time, spread to invade other tissues.

Practical work

Use a J-tube to analyse air samples:
- determine the percentage oxygen consumption and percentage carbon dioxide consumption of samples of inspired and expired air

Understand the use of a simple respirometer:
- measure oxygen consumption (with potassium hydroxide present)
- measure the net difference between carbon dioxide production and oxygen consumption (in the absence of potassium hydroxide) and so determine carbon dioxide production

Understand the use of the Audus apparatus (photosynthometer):
● the effect of light intensity on the photosynthetic production of oxygen

Demonstrate a compensation point:
● use of bicarbonate indicator

● Gas exchange is most efficient when the exchange surface has a large area, a large diffusion gradient is maintained and the barrier to diffusion is thin.

● Gas exchange in plants is involved in both respiration and photosynthesis.

● In plants, during the night (when only respiration can take place) oxygen is absorbed and carbon dioxide is released. During the day, when the rate of photosynthesis exceeds the rate of respiration, carbon dioxide is absorbed and oxygen is released.

● In plant leaves, the mesophyll is the main gas exchange surface. It has a large surface area, is thin, has an extensive air-space system connected to the atmosphere by stomata that allow the entry of air to maintain a concentration difference.

● In mammals (humans), the alveoli in the lungs are the specialised gas exchange surface through which oxygen diffuses into the blood and carbon dioxide diffuses out.

● The millions of sac-like alveoli provide a large surface area.

● The extremely thin walls of the alveoli and the capillaries (consisting only of squamous epithelium) provide a short diffusion distance.

● The ventilation of the lungs and the circulation of blood across the alveolar surface both maintain high concentration gradients between the alveolar air and the blood.

● Ventilation (inhalation and exhalation) occur because breathing movements create pressure differences between the atmosphere and the air in the lungs. Inhalation involves the contraction of the external intercostal muscles and the diaphragm muscle, so increasing the volume of the thorax and decreasing pressure; exhalation involves the relaxation of these muscles and the recoil of elastic alveoli.

● A number of diseases are associated with smoking: chronic obstructive pulmonary disease, which is a combination of chronic bronchitis and emphysema; and lung cancer.

Summary

Transport and transpiration in flowering plants

Vascular tissues

There are two transport systems in flowering plants:
● **xylem** for water and inorganic ions
● **phloem** for organic molecules, such as sucrose and amino acids

Examiner tip

You should understand why plants need transport systems. Diffusion is too slow to supply the needs of multicellular plants, so mass flow is required. Plants have evolved two distinct systems of tubes: xylem and phloem.

These systems are contained within the plant's **vascular tissues**. Vascular tissues form a central **stele** (vascular cylinder) in the root, but peripheral **vascular bundles** in the stem. In the leaf, vascular tissues form a central large vascular bundle (midrib) from which smaller vascular bundles (veins) run through the leaf.

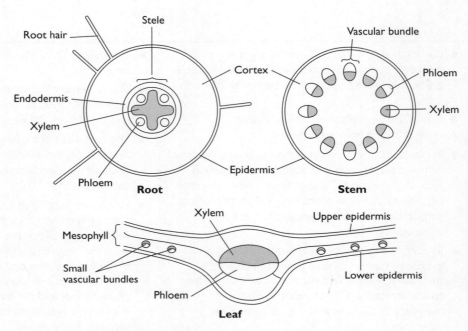

Figure 13 The distribution of vascular tissue (xylem and phloem) in cross sections of root, stem and leaf

Knowledge check 15

Describe the distribution of (a) xylem and (b) phloem in both roots and stems.

Xylem

There are several different types of cell in xylem. The cells that transport most of the water and ions are called **xylem vessels**. In these cells, a secondary wall, impregnated with **lignin,** is formed inside the primary cellulose wall. Lignin is impermeable to water, so mature xylem vessels are dead.

Examiner tip
You may be asked to explain why xylem vessels are lignified. Do not say that it strengthens the xylem vessels; its primary role is to prevent the xylem vessels collapsing under the negative pressures (tension) created as a result of transpiration. A secondary function of lignin is that it offers support to the plant.

There are different patterns of lignification in xylem vessels (Figure 14). In the first formed xylem, known as the **protoxylem**, produced in the growing regions behind the root and shoot tips, an **annular** or **spiral** pattern is produced. These patterns allow the vessels to elongate along with other tissues in the growth regions. In the xylem produced in the mature parts of the plant, known as the **metaxylem**, there is a greater deposition of lignin and a **reticulated** or **pitted** pattern is produced. Reticulated vessels are thickened by interconnecting bars of lignin; pitted vessels are uniformly thickened, except at pores seen as pits that allow rapid movement of water and ions out of the vessels to surrounding cells. The role of the lignin is to prevent the vessels from collapsing when under tension. As the vessels form their end-walls break down, so continuous tubes are formed. As a result, water movement through xylem vessels requires less pressure than through living cells where movement would be slowed down by cell contents.

Thin cell wall is stretched as the plant grows

Rings of lignified cell wall to provide support and prevent collapse

No cell contents — an empty tube gives little resistance to the flow of water

Large empty lumen allows flow of large volumes of water

Thick cell wall — strengthened with lignin to withstand tension and prevent vessel from collapsing

Pits in the cell wall allow water to flow laterally between xylem vessels and to surrounding cells

Annular Spiral Reticulate Pitted

Figure 14 Different patterns of lignification in xylem vessels

Knowledge check 16

List four features of xylem that make it well adapted to the transport of water.

Phloem

Phloem tissue consists of different cell types (Figure 15). The transporting cells are the **sieve tube elements**. These lie end-to-end to form a continuous stack — the sieve tube. The thin cellulose walls at the ends of the cells are perforated to form **sieve plates**, so making movement between sieve tube elements easier. **Companion cells** are closely associated with the sieve tube elements. The cytoplasm of the companion cell is linked via plasmodesmata to that of the sieve tube element. The smaller companion cells have a dense cytoplasm with a large number of mitochondria and have high levels of metabolic activity (see p. 27). They do not transport materials but maintain the activity of the sieve tube elements. This is important since sieve tube elements lose their nuclei and many organelles as they mature.

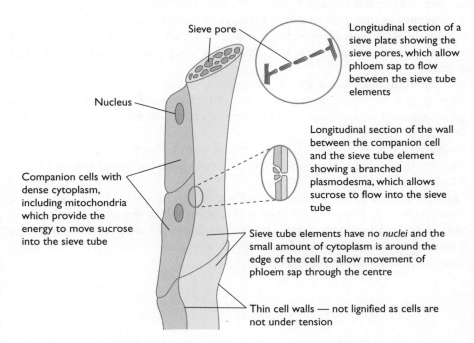

Sieve pore

Longitudinal section of a sieve plate showing the sieve pores, which allow phloem sap to flow between the sieve tube elements

Nucleus

Longitudinal section of the wall between the companion cell and the sieve tube element showing a branched plasmodesma, which allows sucrose to flow into the sieve tube

Companion cells with dense cytoplasm, including mitochondria which provide the energy to move sucrose into the sieve tube

Sieve tube elements have no *nuclei* and the small amount of cytoplasm is around the edge of the cell to allow movement of phloem sap through the centre

Thin cell walls — not lignified as cells are not under tension

Figure 15 Phloem sieve tube and companion cells

Knowledge check 17

Explain the role of companion cells in translocation.

Transpiration and the movement of water and ions

Transpiration is the term used to define the process whereby water vapour is lost from plants (Figure 16). One of the main functions of the waxy cuticle is to waterproof the leaf's surface and so reduce the evaporation of water from the cells of the epidermis. While being an efficient barrier, the cuticle is not impermeable to the passage of water and some water is lost by **cuticular transpiration**. However, water evaporates readily from the cell walls of the mesophyll cells, and so water vapour accumulates in the air spaces. Stomata are closed at night, so little of this water vapour escapes. During the day, the stomata are open to allow the inward diffusion of carbon dioxide for photosynthesis. As a consequence, water vapour diffuses out. This **stomatal transpiration** is the combined effect of evaporation from the mesophyll surface and the diffusion of water vapour out of the open stomata. Stomatal transpiration accounts for 90% or more of all water loss in most plant species.

Internal factors that affect the rate of transpiration are:

- leaf surface area — increased surface area increases the rate of transpiration because more surface with stomata is exposed to the air
- stomatal density — the greater the density, the more stomata (per unit area) there are for water to diffuse out of the leaf
- cuticle thickness — the thicker the cuticle, the more effective it is at waterproofing and, therefore, reducing cuticular transpiration.

A number of **external factors** influence transpiration rate:

- **Temperature** High temperatures increase the transpiration rate in two ways: greater heat energy increases the evaporation of water from the walls of mesophyll cells and increases the diffusion of water molecules out of the open stomata.
- **Air movements** Increased air movement outside the leaf increases the transpiration rate by blowing away the diffusion shells of water vapour that gather outside the open stomata. This increases the water potential gradient out of the leaf.
- **Humidity** Increased humidity decreases the rate of transpiration because when the atmosphere holds more water molecules the water potential gradient to the outside is reduced.
- **Light** Transpiration occurs more quickly in bright light than in the dark since stomata, the major route by which water vapour is lost, are open.
- **Soil water availability** If water is in short supply, plants are unable to replace the water lost in transpiration with water from the soil, and the stomata close, which reduces water loss by transpiration

As the water evaporates from the mesophyll cell walls it is replaced by water from the xylem vessels in the leaf. The flow of water through the mesophyll occurs by two main pathways:

- the **apoplast pathway** — water moves along the cellulose fibrils of the cell walls
- the **symplast pathway** — water diffuses from cell cytoplasm to cell cytoplasm through the plasmodesmata

Most of the water follows the apoplast pathway since this offers least resistance.

As water is drawn out of the xylem vessels, a **tension** (negative pressure) develops and a **water potential gradient** is established through the plant. Water moves through the plant because of this water potential gradient and because of **cohesive forces** between water molecules — the water column in the xylem vessel moves 'as one'. Further, there are **adhesive forces** between water and the cell walls, which tend to prevent the water column dropping down under gravity. This mechanism of water movement through the plant is known as the **cohesion-tension theory**. The pull caused by transpiration is great enough to cause the circumference of a tree to become smaller when transpiration is at its maximum (i.e. midday).

Water and ions are taken up at the root epidermis, where the root hair cells greatly increase the surface area. There are two routes:

- Water is absorbed into the root hair cells by osmosis; ions are absorbed by active transport (or, if the diffusion gradient is favourable, by facilitated diffusion). Subsequent movement across the cortex is along the symplast pathway.
- Water and ions are adsorbed onto the cellulose fibrils of the cell walls. Subsequent movement across the cortex is along the apoplast pathway.

Transport of water across the cells of the **cortex** of the root occurs in the same way as transport through the mesophyll of the leaf, i.e. mostly by the apoplast pathway and some by the symplast pathway. However, the cells of the **endodermis** have a **Casparian strip** that completely encircles each cell and is impermeable to water. This is a barrier to the apoplast pathway, so water can *only travel via the symplast pathway into xylem vessels*. This allows active control of the passage of water and dissolved ions. Ions are pumped by the cytoplasm of the endodermal cells into the xylem and water follows along the resultant water potential gradient, thus creating **root pressure**. Water also moves into the xylem due to the transpirational pull.

Knowledge check 18

Explain why a lack of oxygen reduces ion uptake.

Knowledge check 19

Explain why a respiratory poison would reduce the effect of the root pressure.

Examiner tip

Always refer to water diffusing down a water potential gradient — *never* use the phrase 'water concentration gradient'. Water diffuses through the root cortex, moves up the xylem, and diffuses as water vapour out of the stomata — in each case from a region of higher water potential (less negative) to a region of lower water potential (more negative).

Examiner tip

Transpiration represents a loss of water to the plant. This is only a problem if the loss is excessive or if soil water becomes unavailable, as in a drought. Transpiration is the major force drawing water (which contains dissolved ions) up the plant and it therefore results in a continuous supply of ions for use in the leaf.

Figure 16 The movement of water through a plant

The movement of water out of a leaf, across a root and ultimately through the whole plant is shown in Figure 16, along with the water potential gradient from soil (less negative ψ) to air (more negative ψ).

Xerophytes

Xerophytes are plants that are adapted to living in dry habitats. Some of the features that enable plants to tolerate these dry habitats are summarised in Table 3.

Table 3 Summary of some xerophytic features

Features	Advantage of feature
Thick cuticle	Increases the efficiency of the waterproofing layer
Few stomata, leaf very small or with a reduced surface area-to-volume ratio	Reduced pathway for water loss
Stomata sunken into leaf; leaf covered by hairs; leaf rolled with stomata on the inside	Humid air builds up immediately outside the stomata reducing the diffusion gradient out of the leaf
Water storage cells in leaf or stem — succulence	Greater storage of water for use during periods of drought
Leaves adapted as spines	Spines prevent grazing and the exposure of plant tissue to evaporation
Extensive shallow root network or deep network of roots	Greater uptake of water when it does become available

Translocation of organic solutes

The movement of organic solutes within the phloem sap is known as **translocation**. Phloem sap contains primarily **sucrose** (the transport carbohydrate in plants), though amino acids and other solutes are also present. There are two main principles with respect to movement of phloem sap:

- Movement involves **energy expenditure**. There are several lines of evidence that mass flow is maintained by an active mechanism:
  - The rate of flow ($1\,m\,h^{-1}$) is higher than can be accounted for by diffusion.
  - Companion cells have a particularly high density of mitochondria and are more metabolically active than other plant cells. ATP is used to pump sucrose into companion cells from where it enters the sieve tube element via plasmodesmata.
  - Metabolic poisons (e.g. potassium cyanide), which stop respiration, also stop translocation.

- Movement is **two-way** or, more precisely, movement occurs from '**source to sink**'. The source is the organ where sugar is produced in photosynthesis or by the breakdown of starch (e.g. leaves) and the sink is the organ that consumes or stores carbohydrate (developing buds, flowers, fruit, roots and root storage organs). So sugar can be moved up to a developing bud at the shoot tip or down to the roots. Furthermore, source and sink depend on the season: a potato tuber is a sink as it builds up stores of carbohydrate in the summer but is a source in the spring when starch is broken down to supply the energy for the growth of shoots. Evidence for two-way flow comes from the use of radioactively labelled sucrose: following the supply of labelled sucrose to a mature leaf, radioactivity is detected in the shoot tip above and in the roots below.

Knowledge check 20

With reference to the water potential gradient, explain how sunken stomata reduce transpiration.

Examiner tip

The transport of water is a passive process, whereas the transport of organic solutes is an active process.

Knowledge check 21

Experiments with labelled sucrose show that radioactivity is detected in very young leaves but not in mature leaves. Explain why.

Examiner tip

You are not required to give details of any of the theories of translocation.

Examiner tip

The topic of plant transport lends itself to the interpretation and/or drawing of photographs — for example, a section through a root or the stele, a section through the stem or a vascular bundle or a section through a xerophytic leaf. You should examine photographs and/or microscope slides in your revision of roots, stems and leaves.

Practical work

Demonstration of a bubble 'potometer' and its use in measurement of the rate of water uptake:

● use to measure rate of water uptake
● use to investigate external factors that influence the rate of transpiration

- Flowering plants have two transport (vascular) systems: xylem and phloem.
- In roots, xylem and phloem are found in a central vascular cylinder or stele; in stems, they are found in radially arranged vascular bundles that branch into the leaves.
- In xylem, water and ions are transported in vessels that are well adapted for this function — no cross walls or cytoplasm (to impede movement), lignified (to prevent collapse) but with pores (to allow water to move out laterally).
- Water and ions are absorbed by root hairs, which have a large surface area, and are passed across the root cortex by the apoplast and symplast pathways.
- At the endodermis that lines the stele, water and ions are forced to enter the cytoplasm (symplast pathway). From here ions are pumped into the xylem so that water follows osmotically, creating root pressure.
- Xylem carries water and ions from the roots through the stem to the leaves — it is one-way flow.
- Water is lost from the leaves by the process of transpiration, whereby water evaporates from the mesophyll surface and diffuses out, mainly through open stomata.

- Transpiration is influenced by internal factors (e.g. stomatal density and cuticle thickness) and external factors (e.g. temperature, air movement, humidity and light).
- Xerophytes have adaptations that reduce transpiration.
- Transpiration creates a negative pressure (tension) in the leaf xylem and is the major force drawing water up, supported by the combined forces of cohesion and adhesion, and to a lesser extent by the root pressure.
- In all cases water moves down a water potential gradient, i.e. from a region of higher water potential to a region of lower (more negative) water potential.
- In phloem, organic solutes (mainly sucrose and amino acids) are transported in sieve tubes. These have reduced cytoplasm and cross walls with pores, the sieve plates, to facilitate movement. Translocation of organic solutes is an active process that relies on the metabolism of adjacent companion cells.
- Phloem carries organic solutes from the 'source' of sugar (mature leaves) to the 'sinks' (roots and growth areas).

Blood transport system in mammals

The mammalian circulatory system

Knowledge check 22

Explain why large, active animals need a transport system.

In mammals, during one complete pathway around the body, the blood flows through the heart twice. One circuit going from the heart to the lungs and back is the **pulmonary circulation**. The other circuit from the heart to the rest of the body is the **systemic circulation**. Since there are two circuits, this is called a **double circulatory system**. Blood is pumped twice by the heart, from the *right ventricle to the lungs* and from the *left ventricle to the body*. These two chambers both have thick walls made of cardiac muscle, but the muscle of the left ventricle is thicker than the muscle of the right ventricle. Therefore, the blood pumped by the left ventricle is pushed harder and is under greater pressure than blood from the right ventricle. This two-pressure system has advantages:

- The low pressure in the pulmonary circulation pushes blood slowly to the lungs allowing more time for gas exchange.
- The high pressure in the systemic circulation ensures blood is pumped to all the other body organs and allows tissue fluid to form in each organ.

An artery branches off the systemic circulation to supply each of the body organs and a vein returns the blood to the heart. The main blood vessels of the thorax and abdomen are shown in Figure 17.

Knowledge check 23

What are the advantages of a double circulatory system over a single circulatory system?

Figure 17 The double circulatory system showing the main blood vessels

Examiner tip
You are required to name only the main blood vessels, as shown in Figure 17.

Knowledge check 24

Describe the pathway that blood takes between the vena cava and the aorta.

Figure 18 Coronary arteries supply blood to the heart muscle

The heart needs its own supply of blood — the coronary circulation — to provide cardiac muscle with oxygen and nutrients. The coronary arteries arise from the base of the aorta. Problems may occur in branches of the coronary arteries (see pp. 40–41).

The heart

The structure of the heart

The structure of the heart with its associated blood vessels is shown in Figure 19.

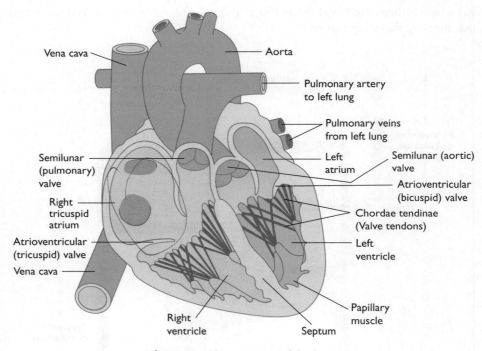

Figure 19 The structure of the heart

Examiner tip
The two-pressure system is caused by the difference in thickness of the muscle of the ventricle walls. The thicker left ventricle muscle creates the higher pressure needed to send blood to the body cells; the thinner right ventricle muscle produces the lower pressure to the lungs.

The cardiac cycle

There are three main stages during each beat of the heart:

- **atrial systole** — atria contract (ventricles are relaxed)
- **ventricular systole** — ventricles contract (atria are relaxed)
- **diastole** — both atria and ventricles are relaxed

These stages occur at the same time in the right and left sides of the heart.

The **pressure changes** in the left atrium, the left ventricle and in the aorta during one cardiac cycle are shown in Figure 20 on p. 32.

A graph of the changes in the right atrium, right ventricle and pulmonary artery shows all the same features, but the pressures in the right ventricle and pulmonary artery are lower.

Knowledge check 25

Why is the maximum pressure similar in both atria?

The sequence of events during each phase of the cardiac cycle is shown in Table 4 on pp. 32–33. The numbers of the stages in Table 4 are also shown in Figure 20.

As valves close, the flaps of tissue snap together making a sound. The first (and softer) heart sound is produced by closure of the atrioventricular valves; the second, sharper sound is produced by the clapping shut of the semilunar valves. These sounds are shown in the **phonocardiogram** in Figure 20 (see p. 32). The electrical activity through the heart is recorded as an **electrocardiogram** and is shown in Figure 20. Wave **P** shows the excitation of the atria, **QRS** indicates the excitation of the ventricles and **T** corresponds to diastole.

Coordination of the cardiac cycle

The sequence of atrial systole, ventricular systole and diastole occurs as a result of coordinated waves of excitation through the heart. The heartbeat is **myogenic** — contraction originates in the heart itself and does not depend on nervous stimulation. The heartbeat starts at the **sinoatrial node** (**SAN**), a small patch of tissue in the right atrium that acts as a **pacemaker**. Excitation from the SAN spreads rapidly over the atria causing them to contract together (atrial systole). Between the atria and the ventricles is a layer of **non-conductive tissue**, which prevents the spread of the wave of excitation passing directly from the atria to the ventricles. The only conducting route for the wave of excitation to the ventricles is via the **atrioventricular node** (**AVN**). Waves of excitation from the SAN reach the AVN and there is a short time delay before the waves of excitation pass down to the base of the ventricles. The AVN is connected to specialised muscle fibres called the **bundle of His**, which transports a wave of excitation down both sides of the septum to the base of the ventricles. Special fibres called **Purkinje fibres** (also known as Purkyně fibres), which branch upwards, conduct the waves of excitation to all parts of the ventricles causing them to contract from the bottom up. This ensures that blood is pushed up from the ventricles into the arteries. The two ventricles contract at exactly the same time (ventricular systole). Once cardiac muscle contracts it goes into a period of rest (diastole) before it can contract again. The waves of excitation through the heart are shown in Figure 21 on p. 33.

Knowledge check 26

List the functions of the SAN, AVN and bundle of His.

Knowledge check 27

Explain the advantage of (a) the delay in the impulses through the AV node, and (b) the ventricles contracting from the base upwards.

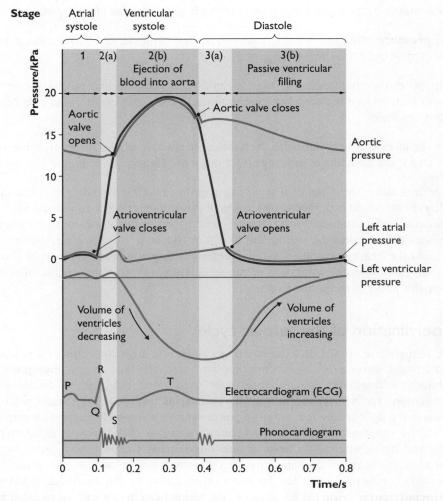

Figure 20 The pressure changes in left atrium, left ventricle and aorta during one cardiac cycle (with ventricular volume changes, electrocardiogram and phonocardiogram)

Knowledge check 28

What causes the atrioventricular valves to close?

Knowledge check 29

During which stage(s) in the cardiac cycle are the semilunar valves closed? Explain your answer.

Table 4 The sequence of events during stages of the cardiac cycle

Stage	Description of events
(1) Atrial systole	Atria contract (ventricles are relaxed) pushing more blood into the ventricles. This is essentially topping up the ventricles (since blood has already entered the ventricles during diastole when the atrioventricular valves are open).
(2) Ventricular systole (a)	Ventricles contract (atria are relaxed) causing the pressure of the blood inside the ventricles to become greater and forcing the atrioventricular valves shut. Two phases are evident (see Figure 20): (a) Ventricular pressure causes the atrioventricular valves to bulge into the atria increasing pressure there, while not

Table 4 The sequence of events during stages of the cardiac cycle (*continued*)

Stage	Description of events
(b)	being great enough to cause blood to exit the major arteries; the flaps of the atrioventricular valves are prevented from turning inside out by the chordae tendinae aided by contraction of the papillary muscles (see Figure 19) (b) Ventricular pressure increases to exceed that in the major arteries, pushing the semilunar valves open and causing the ejection of blood from the heart; blood is returned to the atria from the major veins and so atrial pressure gradually increases
(3) Diastole (a) (b)	Cardiac muscle throughout the atria and ventricles relaxes. Two phases are evident (see Figure 20): (a) Ventricular pressure drops to become lower than that in the main arteries so the semilunar valves are forced shut. Blood continues to be returned to the atria though it cannot enter the ventricles since the ventricular pressure is still greater than that in the atria, so atrioventricular valves remain closed. (b) Ventricular pressure drops to a point where it becomes lower than that in the atria. Therefore, the atrioventricular valves are forced open and blood enters the ventricles from the atria.

Examiner tip

You should be able to interpret data showing pressure changes in the heart chambers and major arteries, such as those in Figure 20. You need to work through this graph and recognise the events of the cardiac cycle. Note that blood flows from a region of high pressure to a region of lower pressure, unless prevented from doing so by the forced closure of a valve. When valve flaps snap together a heart sound is made.

Knowledge check 30

Figure 20 shows a heartbeat of duration 0.8 seconds. Calculate the heart rate in beats per minute.

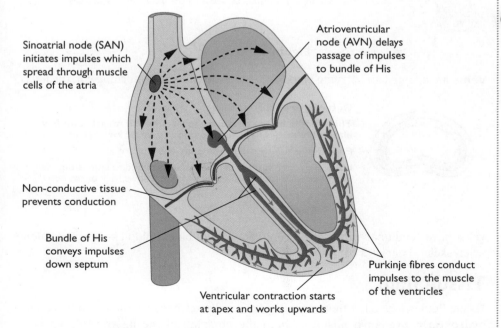

Sinoatrial node (SAN) initiates impulses which spread through muscle cells of the atria

Atrioventricular node (AVN) delays passage of impulses to bundle of His

Non-conductive tissue prevents conduction

Bundle of His conveys impulses down septum

Purkinje fibres conduct impulses to the muscle of the ventricles

Ventricular contraction starts at apex and works upwards

Figure 21 The waves of excitation through the heart

The blood vessels

Arteries are adapted for carrying blood under high pressure away from the heart, towards individual organs.

Examiner tip

Do *not* say that the muscle in arterial walls is used to push the blood along. Its contraction *constricts* (narrows) the artery.

Knowledge check 31

Which possesses more elastic tissue, the aorta or the pulmonary artery? Explain your answer.

Examiner tip

You should be able to list all the adaptations of capillaries for their role in the exchange of substances: thin wall made of squamous epithelium, permeable to water and solutes; large surface area for diffusion; capillaries are close to body cells; blood flows slowly, giving time for diffusion; capillaries are more extensive in organs where the metabolic rate is high.

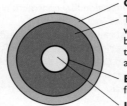

Outer layer of fibrous tissue — protection

Thick middle layer containing elastic tissue — allows stretching when blood surges (during systole) and recoils to continue pushing blood along (during diastole) — and **muscle tissue** — may contract to narrow the lumen (vasoconstriction) so reducing blood supply to an organ, or relax to increase supply (vasodilation)

Endothelium — provides a smooth inner surface which reduces the friction caused by blood flow through the lumen

Lumen — small, maintaining a high blood pressure, and may be constricted or dilated

Figure 22 The wall of an artery

Note that the muscle in arterial walls is *not* used to push the blood along.

Capillaries are adapted for the exchange of material between the blood and the tissue cells. The vast networks of capillaries slow the blood, giving time for the diffusion to occur.

The fluid that leaks out of the capillaries is called **tissue fluid**. It bathes all the surrounding cells. Polymorphs and monocytes, two types of white blood cell, can also leave the capillaries, squeezing between adjacent endothelial cells, at sites of infection.

Squamous (pavement) endothelium — thin wall, permeable to water and solutes, so providing a short diffusion distance and facilitating the exchange of substances between the blood and tissue cells

Figure 23 A capillary

Veins are adapted for carrying blood under low pressure and returning it to the heart.

Outer layer of fibrous tissue — protection

Thin middle layer containing some smooth muscle and few elastic fibres — small layer since blood is under low pressure

Endothelium — provides a smooth inner surface

Lumen — large space making it easier for blood to enter from the capillaries while friction is reduced as blood flows back to the heart

Figure 24 The wall of a vein

Veins have semilunar valves to prevent backflow of blood. Blood is squeezed along when skeletal muscles contract.

Tissue fluid

Tissue fluid is formed at the arterial end of capillaries because the blood has a high **hydrostatic pressure** (resulting from the pumping of the heart). This pressure forces plasma minus its proteins out of the capillaries (proteins are too big to filter out) and is only partly resisted by the low solute potential of the blood (resulting from the retention of proteins). Tissue fluid carries glucose, ions and oxygen to the cells. The loss of fluid from the capillaries reduces the hydrostatic pressure of the blood. Therefore, at the venous end, due to the low solute potential of the blood, fluid (i.e. water, carbon dioxide and other waste products) is drawn into the capillaries by osmosis and diffusion.

Blood

Blood is a suspension of cells in a pale yellow liquid called **plasma**.

Blood cells

Erythrocytes (red blood cells) are much more numerous than white blood cells, of which there are different types — **polymorphs**, **monocytes** and **lymphocytes**. A drawing of a blood smear containing these cell types is shown in Figure 25.

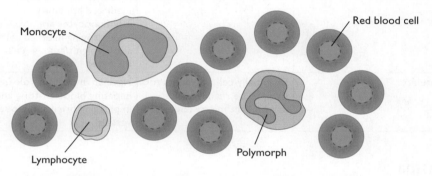

Figure 25 A drawing of the different cell types in a blood smear

The structure and function of blood cells is summarised in Table 5.

Table 5 A summary of the structure and function of different blood cells

Cell type	Structure	Function
Erythrocytes (red blood cells)	Small (diameter 7–8 µm) cells lacking a nucleus and organelles, and with a biconcave disc shape. They are packed with haemoglobin.	The cells are adapted for the carriage of oxygen. The lack of a nucleus provides even more space for haemoglobin, an oxygen-carrying red pigment. The biconcave disc shape increases the surface area over which gas exchange can occur.
Polymorphs	Cells (diameter 10–12 µm) with a multilobed nucleus and granular cytoplasm. They are the most common white blood cell (70%).	These short-lived, but numerous cells can squeeze between the endothelial cells of the capillaries at sites of infection where they engulf bacteria and other foreign bodies by phagocytosis.

Knowledge check 32

State where red blood cells 'pick up' oxygen and where they are likely to release it again.

Knowledge check 33

How is a red blood cell adapted to carry haemoglobin and facilitate its functioning in oxygen transport?

Table 5 A summary of the structure and function of different blood cells (*continued*)

Cell type	Structure	Function
Monocytes	Large cells (diameter 14–17 μm) with a kidney-shaped nucleus. The least common white blood cell (5%).	They reside in the blood for only a few days before moving out into the tissues of body organs where they develop into macrophages, which are long-lived phagocytic cells that engulf bacteria and foreign material.
Lymphocytes	Cells (diameter 7–8 μm) with a huge nucleus and little cytoplasm. Present in relatively large numbers (25% of white blood cells).	There are two types of lymphocyte: B lymphocytes are involved in antibody production as part of the immune response — antibody-mediated immunity; T lymphocytes are involved in destroying infected cells and foreign tissue — cell-mediated immunity.
Platelets	Essentially cell fragments too small to be readily visible using a light microscope.	Have an important role in initiating blood clotting and in plugging breaks in blood vessels.

Knowledge check 34

Which white blood cells are involved in phagocytosis? How do they differ in function?

Knowledge check 35

In what form is carbohydrate transported in plants and in animals?

Plasma

Plasma consists of 90% water and 10% of a variety of substances in solution and suspension: plasma proteins including prothrombin and fibrinogen (involved in clotting), albumin and enzymes, hormones, glucose, amino acids, fats and fatty acids, urea (excretory product), vitamins and various ions (e.g. Ca^{2+} as a clotting factor).

Blood clotting

The clotting of blood seals cuts and wounds, preventing the entry of pathogens and stopping the loss of blood. When blood vessels are injured, a chain of reactions is initiated. In the final stages of the process, an inactive plasma protein, **prothrombin**, is converted into active **thrombin**. Thrombin is an enzyme that converts soluble **fibrinogen** into insoluble **fibrin**. The fibrin forms a mesh that traps red blood cells and forms a **clot**. A summary of the sequence of events in clotting is given in Figure 26.

If blood clots too readily then **thrombosis** may occur (an internal clot is called a **thrombus**). This is blood clotting in an unbroken blood vessel, which is dangerous and can lead to a stroke or heart attack. Conversely, if blood takes too long to clot **haemorrhage** may occur. In this case a great deal of blood may be lost from the blood vessels, which is also dangerous. The hereditary disorder **haemophilia** is a condition in which factor VIII is missing from the blood, as a result of which the blood cannot form clots without medical intervention.

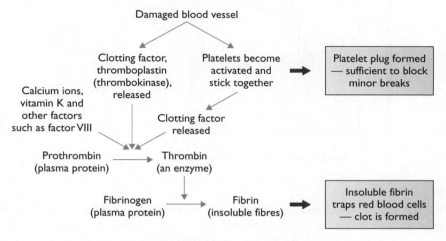

Figure 26 Blood clotting

Knowledge check 36

Name two enzymes involved in clotting and describe their action.

Haemoglobin and the carriage of oxygen

Haemoglobin is a conjugated protein found in large quantities in red blood cells. Each molecule consists of four polypeptides: two α-chains and two β-chains. Each polypeptide has a **haem** group attached, which contains **iron** (Fe^{2+}). An oxygen molecule can associate with each haem to form oxyhaemoglobin.

$$Hb + 4O_2 \rightleftharpoons HbO_8$$
Haemoglobin + oxygen $\rightleftharpoons$ oxyhaemoglobin

The equation shows that one molecule of oxyhaemoglobin can carry up to four molecules of oxygen. It also shows that the reaction is reversible: if oxygen is plentiful, oxyhaemoglobin is produced; if oxygen levels are low, oxyhaemoglobin breaks down (**dissociates**).

Blood contains a vast number of haemoglobin molecules — each mm^3 of blood contains about 5 million red blood cells and each red blood cell contains about 280 million molecules of haemoglobin. The amount of oxygen carried by all this haemoglobin is measured as the degree to which the blood is **saturated** — 50% saturated means that, on average, each haemoglobin molecule is carrying two oxygen molecules. The amount of oxygen carried by the blood depends on the amount of oxygen available in its surroundings. This is measured as its **partial pressure** (abbreviated pO_2), which is the proportion of the total air pressure that is contributed by the oxygen in the mixture. It is measured in kilopascals (kPa). Figure 27 shows the **oxygen dissociation curve** of human haemoglobin. This indicates how the percentage saturation of blood with oxygen changes with the partial pressure of oxygen.

Examiner tip
When considering haemoglobin dissociation curves you should think about what is happening in the body. The partial pressure of oxygen in the lungs is about 14 kPa so haemoglobin 'picks up' (loads with) oxygen; in respiring tissues the partial pressure is approximately 5 kPa so haemoglobin cannot 'hold on' to the oxygen and therefore releases (unloads) it.

Figure 27 The oxygen dissociation curve of human haemoglobin

While the data for the graph are obtained experimentally (by bubbling air of different oxygen partial pressures through blood and measuring the degree to which the blood becomes saturated with oxygen) it provides evidence for what is happening in the body. The partial pressure of oxygen in the alveoli is relatively high (14 kPa). Therefore, since the blood entering the pulmonary circulation is deoxygenated, the haemoglobin **loads** with oxygen to become 98% saturated. In respiring tissues, oxygen is being used up and so the pO_2 is low (5 kPa). At this low pO_2, the blood can only be 70% saturated and, since blood arriving at the tissues is highly saturated, the haemoglobin **unloads** oxygen and so the tissues are supplied with oxygen. During strenuous exercise the pO_2 in muscles is reduced to 3 kPa, at which level the blood can only be 43% saturated, and so even more oxygen is unloaded. (You should use the graph in Figure 27 to go over these numbers.)

A significant feature of the graph in Figure 27 is that it is S-shaped (**sigmoid**). The reason for this relates to the way in which the four haem-containing polypeptides interact. When the first oxygen molecule combines with the first haem group, the shape of the haemoglobin molecule becomes distorted. This makes it easier for the other three oxygen molecules to bind with the other haem groups.

The amount of oxygen carried by haemoglobin depends not only on the partial pressure of oxygen but also on the **partial pressure of carbon dioxide (pCO_2)**. The effect of carbon dioxide on the oxygen dissociation curve of human haemoglobin is shown in Figure 28. This shows that at higher carbon dioxide partial pressures, the oxygen dissociation curve moves to the right. This is known as the **Bohr effect**.

The Bohr effect increases the efficiency of haemoglobin for oxygen transport. The partial pressure of carbon dioxide is high in tissues that are actively respiring (e.g. muscle). The higher the level of carbon dioxide, the lower the affinity of haemoglobin for oxygen, and so more oxygen is released to the tissues. This is advantageous because tissues with a high respiration rate require increased amounts of oxygen. In the alveoli the partial pressure of carbon dioxide is low (since it is breathed out), and so the affinity of haemoglobin for oxygen is increased and more oxygen can be loaded. This is advantageous because it allows the blood to become as fully saturated as possible.

Figure 28 The effect of carbon dioxide on the oxygen dissociation curve of human haemoglobin

Knowledge check 37

Explain how haemoglobin supplies more oxygen to actively respiring tissues than to those that have a low level of respiration.

Higher temperature and lower pH also have a Bohr effect: exercising muscle generates more heat and, as the temperature in the muscle increases, more oxygen is released.

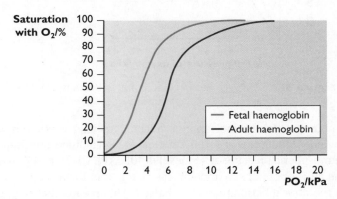

Figure 29 The oxygen dissociation curves for fetal and adult haemoglobin

Knowledge check 38

Figure 29 shows the dissociation curves for fetal and adult haemoglobin.

Explain why fetal haemoglobin must have a higher affinity for oxygen than adult haemoglobin.

Myoglobin is not a blood pigment, but is found in 'red' muscle. It consists of one polypeptide with a single haem group, and does not, therefore, have a sigmoid dissociation curve. Myoglobin has a very high affinity for oxygen, as shown in Figure 29.

Figure 30 The oxygen dissociation curve of myoglobin compared with that of haemoglobin

Myoglobin only releases oxygen when the partial pressure of oxygen in the tissues becomes very low. It acts as an **oxygen store** within the muscle. If, as a result of strenuous exercise, the pO_2 becomes very low then myoglobin gives up its oxygen. This enables aerobic respiration to continue for longer and delays the onset of anaerobic respiration.

Oxyhaemoglobin dissociation curves for different species show considerable differences. For example, the oxygen dissociation curve for llama haemoglobin shows it to have a particularly high affinity for oxygen (see Figure 31).

Figure 31 The oxygen dissociation curve of llama haemoglobin compared with that of human haemoglobin

Examiner tip

Animals that live in oxygen-limited environments have haemoglobin with a high affinity for oxygen. Examples include the prairie dog, a North American burrowing rodent that spends long periods in underground burrows; the Tibetan bar-headed goose which, during migration, flies over the Himalayas; the tench, a fish often found in less well-oxygenated waters. You must be ready to interpret any situation with which you are presented.

The llama, a mammal of the camel family, is adapted to living at altitudes of about 5000 metres in the Andes Mountains of South America. At high altitude, atmospheric pressure is low. The atmospheric pressure at sea level is 101.3 kPa so, with 21% oxygen present, the pO_2 in the air is about 21 kPa, though less at 14 kPa in the alveoli. At an altitude of 5500 metres the atmospheric pressure is halved. This means that pO_2 is reduced to 10.5 kPa and the alveolar pO_2 is only 7 kPa. The llama haemoglobin has a **high oxygen affinity** so that the blood can become fully saturated with oxygen at lower pO_2.

Human haemoglobin is not fully saturated at high altitude and an unacclimatised person would begin to show signs of lack of oxygen — breathlessness, headache, nausea and fatigue (mountain sickness). However, a person who moves to high altitude gradually, will, after 2–3 days, begin to become **acclimatised**. One of the most obvious changes is an increased production of red blood cells. Thus, there is a greater capacity for carrying oxygen to compensate for the lower levels of oxygen available. This response has been used by endurance athletes to increase their potential for oxygen delivery to the muscles when they compete subsequently at low altitude. However, the situation is not simple — for example, the quality of any training is reduced and must be less intense because of the lack of oxygen at high altitude.

Cardiovascular disease

Atherosclerosis

Atherosclerosis is a disease in which an artery wall thickens as a result of a build-up of fatty materials. Risk factors include smoking, inactivity, stress, salt intake, high blood cholesterol and alcohol consumption. The process involves the following sequence of events:

(1) The endothelium lining the artery becomes damaged. This damage can result from **high blood pressure**, which puts an extra strain on the layer of cells, or it might result from toxins from tobacco smoke in the bloodstream.

(2) Once the endothelium is breached there is an inflammatory response. Macrophages (derived from monocytes) leave the blood vessel and move into the artery wall. These cells accumulate chemicals from the blood, particularly **cholesterol**. A deposit builds up, which is called an **atheroma**.

(3) Calcium salts and fibrous tissue also build up at the site, resulting in a hard swelling called a **plaque** on the inner wall of the artery. The build-up of fibrous tissue means that the artery wall loses some of its elasticity — the artery is said to 'harden'. Atherosclerosis is often referred to as 'hardening of the arteries'.

(4) Plaques cause the artery to become narrow and, due to loss of elasticity, the artery is less compliant (i.e. unable to dilate or constrict). This makes it difficult for the heart to pump blood around the body and can lead to a rise in blood pressure. Raised blood pressure makes it more likely that further plaques will form.

If the arteries become very narrow or completely blocked then they cannot supply enough blood.

Examiner tip

If asked to describe atheroma formation, make sure that you refer to an accumulation of materials *within* the artery wall and not on its inner surface.

Coronary thrombosis

If a fatty plaque in an artery ruptures cholesterol is released, which leads to rapid clot formation. A clot that forms inside a damaged, but intact, blood vessel is called a **thrombus** and the condition is called **thrombosis**. If this happens in the **coronary arteries** it is called a **coronary thrombosis**. The heart muscle supplied by these arteries does not receive any oxygen. If the affected muscle cells are starved of oxygen for long they will be damaged permanently. This results in a heart attack or **myocardial infarction**. If a small branch of an artery is blocked only a small amount of muscle dies, causing a small heart attack; if a large artery is blocked, the whole heart may stop beating — a **cardiac arrest** (see Figure 32).

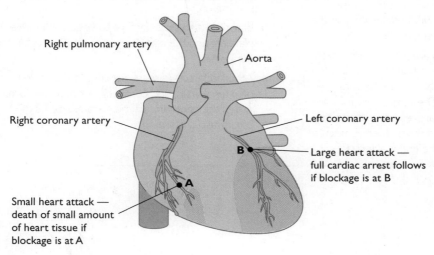

Figure 32 Different-sized heart attacks

Practical work

Examine prepared slides and/or photographs of blood vessels (in section) and mammalian heart (dissected and in section):

- distinguish between arteries, veins and capillaries
- identify heart chambers, atrioventricular valves, semilunar valves, chordae tendinae, papillary muscles, interventricular septum, major blood vessels (vena cavae, pulmonary arteries and aorta)

Examine stained blood films using the light microscope and/or photographs:

- identify erythrocytes, polymorphs, monocytes, lymphocytes and platelets

Summary

- Mammals have a double circulatory system. Blood is pumped to the pulmonary circulation from the right ventricle and returns from the lungs to the left atrium. It is pumped to the systemic circulation from the left ventricle and returns from the body to the right atrium.

- There are three stages to the cardiac cycle:
  - diastole, when all heart muscle is relaxed with blood returning to the atria and flowing into the ventricles
  - atrial systole, when the atrial muscle contracts to 'top-up' the ventricles
  - ventricular systole, when ventricular muscle contracts to force blood into the major arteries (pulmonary artery from the right ventricle and aorta from the left ventricle)

- The heart is myogenic. Excitation originates at the SAN (the pacemaker) and spreads to the AVN before passing down the bundle of His and up the walls of the ventricles via Purkinje fibres.

- The atrioventricular valves are forced open when pressure in the atria exceeds that in the ventricles and forced closed when pressure in the ventricles exceeds that in the atria. The semilunar valves are forced closed when arterial pressure exceeds that in the ventricles and forced open when ventricular pressure exceeds that in the major arteries.

- Arteries are adapted to carry blood away from the heart, under high pressure, to the organs. Veins are adapted to return blood, under low pressure, to the heart.

- Exchange takes place in the capillaries within organs, with tissue fluid carrying substances (e.g. oxygen and glucose) to the cells.

- Blood consists of plasma and cells:
  - red blood cells to carry haemoglobin
  - lymphocytes to form B and T cells in the immune response to antigens
  - polymorphs and macrophages (formed from monocytes) to carry out phagocytosis

- Haemoglobin is adapted to 'pick-up' oxygen at high pO_2 (in lungs) and release it at low pO_2 (in respiring tissue). Further dissociation of oxygen takes place if the pCO_2 is increased as a result of increased respiration.

- Blood clotting seals damage to vessels. It involves platelets and the plasma proteins, prothrombin and fibrinogen.

- Atherosclerosis (disease resulting in the thickening of arterial walls) and coronary thrombosis (clotting within the coronary arteries) are examples of cardiovascular disease.

Diversity of life

Classification

There is such a huge diversity of life on Earth that it makes sense to try to provide some degree of order by categorising the organisms — putting them into groups according to their similarities and differences. This grouping of organisms is known as **classification** and the study of biological classification is called **taxonomy**. Biological classification attempts to classify living organisms according to how closely related they are. It makes use of information from all areas of biology — for example cell structure, immunology, physiology, anatomy, behaviour, life cycles, ecology — and also from biochemistry. The basic unit of biological classification is the **species**.

The concept of the species

A species is defined as 'a group of organisms that is capable of interbreeding to produce viable and fertile offspring'.

This definition attempts to take into account some of the difficulties in describing 'what a species is':

- Robins in Ireland do not interbreed with robins in France, because they are geographically isolated, but they are *capable* of doing so — they are members of the same species.
- A horse and a donkey are capable of interbreeding, but their progeny, the mule, is *sterile* — they are different species.

Members of the same species have numerous features in common while still exhibiting some degree of variation. They have many genes in common, but variation is generated by the alleles that differ.

The number of species on Earth is estimated to be between 3 and 30 million. Only 2 million have so far been identified.

Classifying species

Species are classified into groups or categories of increasing size, i.e. **species**, **genus**, **family**, **order**, **class**, **phylum** and **kingdom**. Each of these groups is called a **taxon** (plural **taxa**). These are shown in Table 6.

Table 6

Taxon	Description
Genus (plural genera)	Group of related species
Family	Group of related genera
Order	Group of related families
Class	Group of related orders
Phylum (plural phyla)	Group of related classes
Kingdom	Group of related phyla

Knowledge check 39

A biologist wished to determine whether the members of two populations belonged to the same species. How could this be achieved?

Examiner tip

Be prepared to place taxa in the correct order. The descending order of **k**ingdom, **p**hylum, **c**lass, **o**rder, **f**amily, **g**enus and **s**pecies can be remembered as '**k**eep **p**ond **c**lean **o**r **f**rog **g**ets **s**ick' (kpcofgs).

Examiner tip

The name given to each species is *both* names in the binomial. The second name should *not* be called the species name. Rather, it is called the specific name, unique to a species within the genus.

Knowledge check 40

Why is it important for scientists to use Latin names, rather than common names, for organisms mentioned in research papers?

The Latin names of all taxa except those of species take initial upper case letters, while anglicised versions do not — for example the kingdom Animalia has members that are called animals.

Naming species

Species are named using the name of their genus and species. This is called the binomial system. By international convention, genus and species names are written in italics (underlined when handwritten); the genus name has an upper case initial letter and the species has a lower case initial letter, e.g. the European robin is named *Erithacus rubecula*. When a binomial has been used once in a passage it may be shortened subsequently (e.g. *E. rubecula*), providing that this does not cause confusion. If the species is not certain but the genus is known, it is possible to refer to an organism by the name of the genus followed by 'sp.' (plural 'spp.') — for example *Littorina* sp., a species of periwinkle.

The five kingdoms

A five kingdom classification system is presently recognised, though new discoveries lead to new ideas and this grouping may change in the future. These five kingdoms are:

- **Animalia**
- **Plantae**
- **Fungi**
- **Protoctista**
- **Prokaryotae**

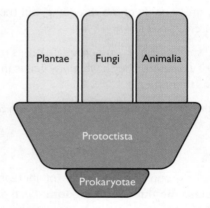

Figure 33 The five kingdom classification

Members of each kingdom have features in common, though some of these are also possessed by members of other kingdoms. For example, members of all the kingdoms except the Prokaryotae have eukaryotic cells. So, while having eukaryotic cells is a feature of the kingdom Plantae, it is *not* a distinguishing feature; members of the kingdom Plantae are distinguished by the possession of cellulose cell walls. Table 7 summarises the features of each of the five kingdoms, with distinguishing features shown in bold.

Table 7 The features of members of each of the five kingdoms

Phylum	Features (distinguishing features in bold)
Animalia	In all cases: multicellular; cells are eukaryotic; cells lack a cell wall. **All animals are heterotrophic** (consuming ready-made organic molecules); **most ingest food into a digestive system.** They store carbohydrates as glycogen; and **usually store lipids as fats.** **Most are capable of locomotion.** Examples include flatworms, segmented worms, arthropods (e.g. insects) and chordates (fish, amphibians, reptiles, birds and mammals).
Plantae	In all cases: they are multicellular; cells are eukaryotic; **cells possess a cellulose cell wall. All plants are photosynthetic, containing chlorophyll in chloroplasts, and are autotrophic (produce all their own food from inorganic material).** They store carbohydrates as starch; and **lipids as oils.** Examples include mosses, ferns, conifers and flowering plants.
Fungi	Fungi are most often multicellular, though a few are unicellular (e.g. yeast). In all cases: cells are eukaryotic (most often organised into filaments, or hyphae, and frequently multinucleate and not divided into separate cells); and **cells have a cell wall, often made of chitin (not cellulose). Fungi have a lysotrophic method of nutrition: they secrete enzymes to digest organic materials (usually dead, but some feed from living hosts) outside their cells and absorb the products of digestion.** They store carbohydrates as glycogen and lipids as oils. Examples include yeast, moulds (e.g. *Mucor*) and toadstools.
Protoctista	This is a diverse group and membership is often by exclusion from all other groups. Some are unicellular, some are filamentous while others are multicellular though show limited differentiation. All protoctistans have eukaryotic cells. Some possess cell walls (cellulose or non-cellulose), chlorophyll (and can photosynthesise); others have no cell walls and are motile. They have a number of different methods of nutrition. Examples include seaweeds (e.g. *Fucus*) and *Amoeba*.

Knowledge check 41

Describe the differences between plants and fungi.

Table 7 The features of members of each of the five kingdoms (continued)

Phylum	Features (distinguishing features in bold)
Prokaryotae	**In all cases: cells are microscopic and prokaryotic: they lack a nucleus and membrane-bound organelles; the DNA is naked and circular; ribosomes are smaller than those of eukaryotes; cell walls are made of peptidoglycans. Since nuclei are lacking, cell division occurs by simple fission.** Different methods of nutrition are exhibited by the prokaryotes. Examples of this highly variable group include bacteria, blue-greens (Cyanobacteria) and hot spring bacteria (belonging to the Archaea group).

Knowledge check 42

Name one characteristic in each of the following kingdoms: (a) fungi; (b) animals.

Knowledge check 43

Apart from being eukaryotic, identify two features that fungi and animals have in common.

Biological classification schemes are devised by taxonomists, based on the best available evidence at the time. New information, in 1990, giving greater weight to findings from molecular biology, has lead to the proposal of a completely new classification. As a result of this information the prokaryotes are now classified as two domains, the Archaea and the Bacteria. All other organisms (i.e. the eukaryotes) are classified within the domain Eukarya.

A phylogenetic classification

The most natural system of classification is one that reflects the ancestral or evolutionary relationships between groups. This system of classification is called **phylogenetic**. It puts the more closely related organisms together into the smaller groups, i.e. genus, then family, etc. Thus, the genus *Panthera* includes the closely related lion (*P. leo*) and tiger (*P. tigris*) but excludes the cheetah (*Acinonyx jubatus*) since it has unique features, although it possesses sufficient similarities to be included within the same family, Felidae.

Usually, the more features in common two species have, the more recently they have evolved from a common ancestor.

With the development of techniques for sequencing the nucleotides in DNA and RNA molecules and the amino acids in proteins, it has become possible to compare organisms at the most basic level — the gene. (Remember that the amino acid sequence in a protein is determined by the nucleotide sequence in a part of the DNA that is acting as a gene.) Closely related organisms are expected to possess a high degree of agreement in the molecular structure of their DNA, RNA and protein; the molecules of organisms related distantly usually show dissimilarity.

Analysis of amino acid differences in proteins, e.g. cytochrome *c*

Protein analysis is used to compare the amino acid sequences of the same protein in different organisms. The more differences, the less closely related the species are presumed to be. Proteins that have been analysed include haemoglobin and cytochrome *c*, which is a protein of about 100 amino acids that is involved in aerobic respiration. Figure 34 shows the number of amino acid differences in the cytochrome *c* of six organisms and the phylogeny based on the cytochrome *c* data. While a classification cannot reliably be based on the analysis of a single protein, the results conform well to phylogenies based on other features.

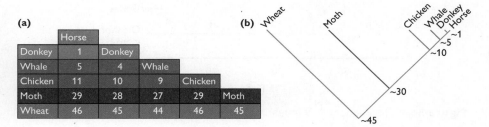

Figure 34 Cytochrome *c* analysis showing (a) the number of amino acid differences of six organisms, and (b) the resultant phylogeny

Analysing protein differences using immunological techniques

The protein albumin is found in the blood plasma of many animals. It is made up of 584 amino acids, although there are differences in the amino acid sequence of the albumin from different species. Without having to obtain the sequences, the differences can be measured using immunological techniques. The principle behind this is that antibodies of one species respond to specific antigens on the proteins, such as albumin, from another species. When antibodies respond to corresponding antigens a precipitate is formed. The greater the degree of precipitation, the closer is the evolutionary relationship. This technique was used to measure how similar human albumin is to albumin from the great apes and from an Old World monkey, the baboon (see Figure 35).

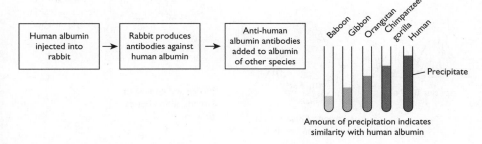

Figure 35 Immunological comparisons of human albumin with that of the great apes

Using this immunological technique, a phylogenetic tree was developed.

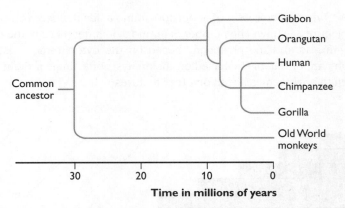

Figure 36 Phylogenetic tree of humans and great apes based on immunological data

Analysing differences in DNA sequences using DNA hybridisation

Comparing DNA sequences is the most accurate way of demonstrating how closely related one species is to another. The greater the similarity between the sequences, the more closely related the two species are. The technique of DNA hybridisation involves extracting samples of DNA from two species, separating the DNA into single strands, mixing these strands and allowing them to re-bind (hybridise). Hybridised strands with a high degree of similarity will re-bind more firmly (see Figure 37).

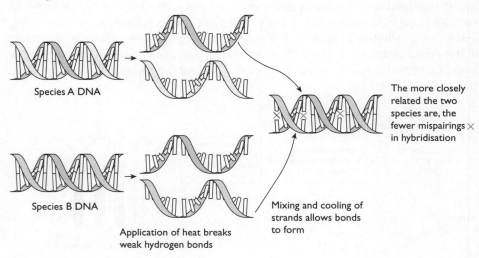

Figure 37 Technique of DNA hybridisation

Samples of DNA from closely related species show a high degree of hybridisation; it is lower for more distantly related species. Using DNA hybridisation techniques, the phylogenetic tree of humans and the great apes appears as in Figure 38.

Figure 38 The phylogenetic tree of humans and the great apes, based on DNA hybridisation data

This is different from, and arguably more accurate than, the tree shown in Figure 36.

Identifying organisms using a key

Identification keys are useful for identifying unfamiliar organisms. They rely on a few, easy-to-see features. The most widely used key, the **dichotomous key**, separates organisms repeatedly into two groups until individual species have been described.

Skills development: construction of a dichotomous key

In an AS2 paper, you could be asked to construct a dichotomous key. A **dichotomous-key question** will probably present you with information about a number of different organisms. A useful starting point is to compile a comparative table of some obvious features shown by some of the organisms (if this has not been done for you in the question). For example, a table comparing four arthropods is shown below.

Feature	Housefly	Butterfly	Spider	Centipede
Segmentation	Yes	Yes	Yes	Yes
Legs	3 pairs	3 pairs	4 pairs	15 pairs
Wings	1 pair	2 pairs	None	None
Antennae	Short and stumpy	Long and club-shaped	None	Long and pointed

You will have decisions to make. Which features should you use to construct the key? In this example, 'segmentation' is of no use since it is common to all the organisms. In fact, only two features are sufficient to construct a dichotomous key. Then you must decide the order in which to use the features — this can be somewhat arbitrary. An example of a dichotomous key is shown below:

(1) Wings present → 2
  Wings absent → 3
(2) One pair of wings — housefly
  Two pairs of wings — butterfly
(3) Four pairs of legs -— spider
  15 pairs of legs — centipede

Guidelines to help you in the construction of keys include:
- Use clearly recognisable features (e.g. number of legs or number of leaflets in a leaf) and avoid those with a range of intermediates (e.g. degree of hairiness).
- Avoid colour and size because these may vary between male and female, adult and juvenile or from season to season.

Examiner tip

You are not expected to know the techniques involved in protein and DNA analysis. However, you are expected to understand the principles and to be able to apply this understanding in answering examination questions.

Knowledge check 44

Why do we need to identify different species in ecological studies?

- Avoid statements such as 'many' or 'few' — 'more than 12' or 'less than 5' are more precise.
- Avoid combining features (e.g. hairy leaves, white flower, stem with a square cross section). Try to keep to one aspect of a single feature (e.g. hairy leaves or leaves not hairy)

Biodiversity

Biodiversity is a contraction of 'biological diversity' and is used to describe the variety of life. It refers to the number *and* variety of organisms within a particular area, and has three components:

- species diversity
- ecosystem (or habitat) diversity
- genetic diversity

Species diversity

Species diversity refers to the number of different species and the numbers of individuals of each species within any one community. A number of objective measures have been created in order to measure species diversity.

Species richness is the number of different species present in an area. The more species present in a sample the 'richer' the area.

Species richness as a measure on its own takes no account of the number of individuals of each species present. **Simpson's index (*D*)** is a measure of diversity that takes into account both species richness and an evenness of abundance among the species present. In essence it measures the probability that two individuals selected randomly from an area will belong to the same species. The formula for calculating *D* is as follows:

$$D = \frac{\sum n_i(n_i - 1)}{N(N - 1)}$$

where $\sum$ = the sum of

n_i = the total number of organisms of each individual species

N = the total number of organisms of all species

The value of *D* ranges from 0 to 1. With this index, 0 represents infinite diversity and, 1, no diversity. That is, the bigger the value of *D*, the lower the diversity.

To calculate Simpson's index for a particular area, the area must be sampled and the number of individuals of each species noted. For example, the diversity of the ground flora in woodland might be determined by sampling with random quadrats. The number of plant species in each quadrat and the number of individuals of each species should be noted. There is no necessity to be able to identify all the species, provided that they can be distinguished from each other. Percentage cover could also be used to determine plant abundance. However, there must be consistency, i.e. either all by 'number of individuals' or all by 'percentage cover'.

Species biodiversity may be used to indicate the 'biological health' of a particular habitat. However, care should be used in interpreting biodiversity measures. Some

Examiner tip

In the exam you could be asked to calculate Simpson's index. The formula for Simpson's index (*D*) will be provided together with the definitions of *n* and *N*. You need to remember that *D* lies between 0 and 1, with a lower number representing greater biodiversity.

habitats are stressful and so few organisms are adapted for life there, but those that are adapted may well be unique or, indeed, rare. Such habitats are important, even if there is little biodiversity. Nevertheless, if a habitat begins suddenly to lose its animal and plant species, ecologists become worried and search for causes, such as a pollution incident. Alternatively, an increase in the biodiversity of an area may mean that corrective measures have been effective.

Ecosystem diversity

This is the **diversity of ecosystems** or habitats within a particular area. A region possessing a wide variety of habitats is preferable and will include a much greater diversity of species than a region in which there are few different habitats. More specifically, countryside that has ponds, river, woodland, hedgerows, wet meadowland and set-aside grassland will be more species rich and more diverse than countryside with ploughed fields, drained land, without wet areas and devoid of woods and hedgerows.

Genetic diversity

This is the **genetic variability** of a species. It refers to the variety of alleles possessed by the individuals that make up any one species. Genetic diversity can be measured directly by genetic fingerprinting or indirectly by observing differences in the physical features of the organisms within the population (e.g. the different colour and banding patterns of the snail *Cepea nemoralis*). Genetic fingerprinting of individuals within cheetah populations has indicated very little genetic variability. Lack of genetic diversity is seen as problematic. It indicates that the species may not have sufficient adaptability and may not be able to survive an environmental hazard. The Irish potato blight of 1846, which resulted in the death of a million people and forced another million to emigrate, was the result of planting only two potato varieties, both of which were vulnerable to the potato blight fungus, *Phytophthora infestans*. The importance of genetic variation is discussed further on p. 55.

Knowledge check 45

Seed banks contain seeds of the ancestors of modern crop plants. Suggest why these seeds are kept.

Summary

- A species (the basic unit of classification) is a group of similar, closely related organisms that are capable of interbreeding with each other to produce viable and fertile offspring.
- Species are classified into groups within a hierarchy. In descending order this hierarchy is: kingdom, phylum, class, order, family, genus, species.
- Species are named according to a binomial system. The genus name is given first, followed by a species name.
- Organisms are grouped into five kingdoms: Prokaryotae (bacteria), Protoctista, Fungi, Plantae, Animalia. Members of the Prokaryotae have prokaryotic cells; members of the other kingdoms have eukaryotic cells.
- A phylogenetic classification is a system that reflects the ancestral or evolutionary relationship between groups.
- Modern methods of establishing relationships include comparison of amino acid sequences in proteins and of nucleotide sequences in DNA and RNA. Closely-related organisms possess a high degree of agreement in the molecular structure of their proteins, DNA and RNA.
- Unfamiliar organisms can be identified using an appropriate dichotomous key.
- Species diversity can be measured by using the Simpson's index (D). Simpson's index (D) values lie between 0 and 1, with values closer to zero indicating greater diversity.
- The 'richness' of a region (such as Northern Ireland) can be described in terms of the diversity of its ecosystems (or habitats).
- Genetic diversity reflects the genetic variability of a species and is important in allowing for the continued adaptability of a species.

Students often have difficulty describing the ecological niche of an organism. What is required is a full description of the environmental requirements for it to survive and reproduce. For example, a fox is a carnivore that hunts mostly at night. However, it may also scavenge; it may compete with other predators (e.g. stoats); it is not predated, though human activities are a major threat (e.g. road deaths); its habitat includes woodland edges where it may dig an 'earth'.

You have met many other examples of adaptation — for example, adaptations of gas exchange surfaces, adaptations in mammals for transporting air in ventilating the lungs and further transporting substances in the blood circulatory system, and the adaptations of the leaf for photosynthesis with prevention of excessive water loss in transpiration.

Explain what is meant by an adaptive feature.

Adaptation of organisms

Organisms live in a **habitat**. They are part of an **ecosystem** within which they interact with both their **biotic** environment (the other living organisms) and with the **abiotic** environment (physical and chemical factors). Members of a single species form a **population** and, with other populations, make up a **community**.

Adaptations

Each organism has an **ecological niche** that describes its role within the ecosystem:

- what it feeds on or other nutrient needs
- what feeds on it
- competition with other organisms
- its temperature, water and other requirements

If it is to survive and reproduce, an organism must have adaptations for each of the above points. Adaptations may be behavioural, physiological or morphological. A **behavioural adaptation** is an aspect of the behaviour of an organism that helps it to survive and reproduce — for example, in attracting a mate. A **physiological** or **biochemical adaptation** is one in which there is appropriate functioning of the organism or its cellular processes — for example, the ability to respire anaerobically. A **morphological** or **anatomical adaptation** refers to any structure that enhances the survival of an organism —for example, the spines on a cactus that prevent grazing.

Adaptations of hydrophytes, plants specifically adapted for living in water, are shown in Figure 8 on p. 16.

Adaptations of xerophytes, plants adapted to living in dry habitats, are summarised in Table 3 (p. 27). This can be further expanded upon:

- Some xerophytes close their stomata when little water is available and some only open their stomata at night, when transpirational loss is reduced. These are behavioural adaptations.
- Some xerophytes possess cells that store water when it is readily available — the plants have succulent leaves and/or stems — for use in times of shortage. This is a physiological adaptation.
- Xerophytes have many morphological or anatomical adaptations such as sunken stomata that trap a layer of moist air next to the stomata, reducing the water potential gradient for water vapour to diffuse into the atmosphere.

Distribution of organisms

The distribution of organisms within their ecosystem is influenced, both separately and jointly, by biotic factors and abiotic factors, the latter being divided into climatic factors and edaphic (soil) factors.

Climatic factors include:

- **Temperature range** The Sun is the main source of heat for ecosystems. The temperature range within which life exists is relatively small. At low temperatures ice crystals may form within cells, causing physical disruption; at high temperatures enzymes are denatured. Fluctuation in environmental temperature is more extreme in terrestrial habitats than aquatic ones because the high heat capacity of water effectively buffers the temperature changes in aquatic habitats.

- **Availability of water** Water is essential to all life and its availability determines the distribution of terrestrial organisms. Many have adaptations to conserve water (e.g. the waxy cuticle of flowering plants and insects); some have less effective waterproofing and so are confined to moist or humid localities (e.g. mosses and woodlice). Even in aquatic habitats there may be problems due to the osmotic movement of water. In marine ecosystems, fish, for example mackerel and pollack, have adaptations to conserve water since there is a tendency for water to be withdrawn osmotically. Some fish (e.g. roach and perch) live exclusively in freshwater and have adaptations to reduce osmotic gain. A few fish (e.g. salmon and eels) are capable of tolerating both extremes during their life cycles.

- **Light intensity** As the ultimate source of energy for ecosystems, light is a fundamental necessity. All plants require light for photosynthesis and most grow better the more light they receive. Some plants, however, are tolerant of low-light conditions, while some (e.g. bluebells) are adapted to grow on the woodland floor before the leaf canopy develops above. In aquatic ecosystems light is absorbed by the water molecules, so aquatic plants and algae can photosynthesise effectively only if they are near the surface. There is even less light in aquatic systems containing suspended particulates such as organic matter.

- **Light quality** Water does not only absorb light, it also influences which wavelengths can penetrate. Blue light penetrates water to a greater depth because red light is absorbed. Some marine algae, the red seaweeds, possess additional red pigments specifically to absorb at the blue end of the spectrum, and so red algae are adapted to live at greater depths than most other algae.

- **Day length** The longer the day length the more time a plant has for photosynthesis. The greater growth of plants in summer is more to do with the increased day length than it is to do with a rise in temperature. Day length also has a role in the flowering of plants.

Edaphic factors include:

- **pH values** The pH of a soil influences the availability of certain ions. Plants such as heathers grow best in acid soils, while spring gentian and cowslip prefer alkaline soils. Species that are tolerant to extremes of pH can become dominant in particular areas because competing species find it hard to survive in these extreme conditions. The dominance of heathers on upland moors is, in part, due to their ability to withstand very low soil pH. However, the optimum pH for the growth of most plants is close to neutral.

- **Availability of nutrients** There is a wide variety of ions required by plants. Some of these are needed in relatively large amounts and are called macronutrients: nitrate for the synthesis of amino acids etc., phosphate for the synthesis of nucleotides etc., calcium for the production of the middle lamella, sulfate for the synthesis of some amino acids and iron for the production of chlorophyll. Some ions are required in minute amounts and are called micronutrients. Different species make different demands on the ions in the soil and therefore plant distribution depends to some extent on the nutrient balance of a particular soil.

- **Water content** The water content of soils varies markedly. It depends on the soil type — clay soils tend to hold a lot of water, sandy soils are freely draining and hold little. A waterlogged soil creates anaerobic conditions. Plants able to tolerate these conditions include the rushes (*Juncus* spp.) and sedges (*Carex* spp.). They have air

> **Knowledge check 47**
> What are edaphic factors?

spaces within their root tissues that allow some diffusion of oxygen from the aerial parts to help supply the roots.
- **Aeration of soils** The space between soil particles is filled with air, from which the roots obtain their respiratory oxygen by diffusion. Soil air is also necessary to the aerobic microorganisms in the soil that decompose the humus.

Biotic factors include:
- **Competitors** Organisms compete with one another when they share a common resource, (e.g. food, water, light or ions) and that resource is in limited supply. They compete not only with members of other species — **interspecific competition** — but also with members of their own species — **intraspecific competition**. Where two species occupy the same ecological niche, the interspecific competition leads to the local extinction of one or the other — the **competitive exclusion principle**.
- **Predators** The distribution of a predator is reliant on the presence of its prey species. The population numbers of both prey and predator are interdependent — when prey numbers are low, predator numbers decline and, when predator numbers become high (due to abundant prey), then prey numbers drop.
- **Accumulation of waste** The growth of microorganisms is frequently self-limiting because the accumulation of waste products can be toxic —for example, in anaerobic conditions yeast populations produce ethanol.

An example of adaptation and distribution: rough and smooth periwinkles

The rough periwinkle (*Littorina saxatilis*) and the common (or edible) periwinkle (*Littorina littorea*) are marine snails found on rocky shores. Both graze algae on rocks and so competition between the two species might be considered to be high. However, the rough periwinkle is found on the upper shore, while the common periwinkle is prevalent in the middle shore. Conditions in the upper and middle shore areas are quite distinct. While the middle shore area is covered by tides for much of the time, the upper shore area is only covered for a few hours each day. Species living on the upper shore must survive the relatively dry conditions and the wide variation in temperatures that is possible. The result is that the two species, while being superficially very similar, possess a distinct series of adaptations to their quite different niches on the shore (Table 8).

Knowledge check 48

Explain the advantage to the rough periwinkle of retaining eggs within its shell and the advantage to the common periwinkle of releasing eggs into the tidal water.

Table 8 Adaptations of the rough and common periwinkle

Adaptation	Rough periwinkle	Common periwinkle
Behavioural adaptation	Sense of orientation that allows them to migrate back to their location on the upper shore if they are swept away by wave action	Able to migrate back to their location in the middle shore if they are swept away by tidal action
Physiological (or biochemical) adaptation	Adults retain fertilised eggs that hatch inside the body and are eventually released as small, shelled copies of the adults — developing eggs are protected from desiccation	Egg capsules are shed into the water, eggs hatch into planktonic larvae (which drift in the tide) and eventually settle on the shore as small, shelled individuals — water is

Adaptation	Rough periwinkle	Common periwinkle
	High temperature tolerance — able to survive the higher air temperatures in summer In extremes of desiccation they cement themselves onto rocks, respiring without oxygen for up to a week Excrete insoluble uric acid so that little water is lost	essential in the reproductive process Not tolerant of wide temperature variation — water temperature does not vary as much as air temperatures Excrete ammonia, which is soluble and must be excreted with lots of water
Morphological (or anatomical) adaptation	Gills are modified to absorb oxygen from air — they are capable of surviving 1 month out of water	Gills are adapted for extracting oxygen from water — they can only breathe for a limited period out of water

Selection of organisms in populations

Environments are not uniform, i.e. factors are not constant throughout any particular habitat. For example, the soil-water content of a meadow may differ with some areas being simply moist and others very wet. (This provides different niches within the habitat and, therefore, areas for different species to survive and reproduce without being in competition.) Furthermore, the light intensity may differ across the meadow because different areas may have a different aspect — for example, some being on a south-facing slope, others facing north. However, populations (of the same species) vary and members of the same population may differ in the extent to which they are adapted to a particular set of conditions. For example, a particular plant species (such as the creeping buttercup, *Ranunculus repens*) may have some members that possess adaptations for very wet conditions while others have a preference for simply moist environments. This variation is genetic and the alleles causing the differences are passed on to any offspring.

There are processes in an organism's life cycle that generate this genetic variation:

- **Meiosis**, through the events of 'independent assortment' and 'crossing-over', produces haploid cells (e.g. gametes in animals), each of which is different from any other (see the AS Unit 1 guide of this series).
- **Cross-fertilisation** brings a set of alleles from one parent into combination with a set of alleles from another parent.

Furthermore, new alleles may be introduced into a population by **mutation** (a spontaneous change in the coding DNA).

Within a *relatively stable environment* (in which conditions are not changing over time) most variations from the norm are selected against. The organisms most likely to reproduce successfully are those with characteristics close to the norm for the population — the **adaptive norm**. This is **stabilising selection**. It reduces the variation for the character since extreme variants are eliminated from the population. As a result, the constancy of the character is maintained.

If gradual *changes occur in the environment over time* the norm for the population may no longer be the most adaptive form. The variants towards one extreme may possess the fitter characteristics, so these are the organisms most likely to survive to reproduce

The adaptiveness of organisms to survive and reproduce is referred to as their **fitness** — defined as the probability that their genes will be passed on to the next generation.

Knowledge check 49

How may genetic variation be increased in (a) sexually reproducing organisms and in (b) asexually reproducing organisms?

Examiner tip

Mutation introduces new alleles into a population on which selection may act. Make sure that you do *not* suggest that the factor creating the selection pressure *causes* the relevant mutation.

Knowledge check 50

Explain why the loss of genetic diversity means that the species can no longer evolve.

Examiner tip

Be careful that you don't suggest that individuals evolve. Individuals are selected and populations evolve.

and pass their genes on to the next generation. This is **directional selection**. There is a shift in the characteristic as different variants are selected for. A change in the genetic composition of the population results, i.e. there is **evolutionary change**. It allows the population to respond to environmental change and remain adaptive.

The two types of selection are described in Figure 39, for a continuous variable exhibiting a normal distribution.

Figure 39 (a) Stabilising selection and (b) directional selection

Stabilising selection can be seen in the selection pressures on human birth weight. Measurements of the survival rate of babies in different weight classes have shown that mortality is highest among the groups weighing much less or much more than the average birth weight.

Knowledge check 51

Explain how some bacteria may become resistant to the antibiotic penicillin.

Examiner tip

When discussing selection and antibiotics, students often state incorrectly that bacteria are *immune* to antibiotics. They become *resistant* to antibiotics.

Directional selection was observed in peppered moths (*Biston betularia*) in Britain during the industrial revolution. Before the industrial revolution changed the environment, the light '*typica*' form was well adapted and the occasional dark '*carbonaria*' form (arising as a result of mutation) was selected against as it lacked camouflage on the lichen-covered trees. The environmental effects of the industrial revolution reversed these selective advantages, so that '*carbonaria*' became the favoured form with the result that its frequency increased in affected populations. Other examples of directional selection have been observed — for example, antibiotic resistance in bacteria, DDT resistance in mosquitoes and warfarin resistance in rats.

Practical work

Describe and carry out qualitative and quantitative techniques used to investigate the distribution and relative abundance of plants and animals in a habitat:
- sampling procedures to include:
  - random sampling
  - line transect
  - belt transect

- sampling devices to include quadrats, pitfall traps, sweep nets and pooters
- estimation of species abundance, density and percentage cover
- appreciation and, where possible, measurement of the biotic and abiotic factors that may be influencing the distribution of organisms

- Each species of organism has an ecological niche — a set of environmental conditions in which it can survive and reproduce.

- Adaptations within an environment may be behavioural, physiological or morphological.

- Hydrophytes are flowering plants adapted for living in water, while xerophytes are plants adapted for living in dry habitats.

- Environmental factors affect the distribution of organisms and include abiotic, climatic and edaphic (soil) factors, and biotic factors.

- Interspecific competition is an important biotic factor. The competitive exclusion principle is that no two species may occupy the same ecological niche.

- Zonation occurs where there is an environmental gradient that affects the distribution of organisms.

- On a rocky shore, rough periwinkles are adapted to the upper shore and common periwinkles are adapted to the middle shore.

- Within sexually reproducing species, genetic variation is generated by the processes of meiosis (crossing over and independent assortment) and cross fertilisation. Mutation occurs in all species and introduces new alleles into the population.

- Genetic variation is acted on by the process of selection, which reduces the range of variation exhibited. The genetic forms selected for are regarded as the 'fittest'. They exhibit better adaptations within their environment, so that they survive to reproduce and pass on their 'fitter' alleles.

- Stabilising selection favours the adaptive norm and selects against extreme variations from the norm. It operates to maintain the constancy of a characteristic in a stable environment.

- Directional selection favours one extreme and selects against the other. It brings about a change in the genetic composition of the population, resulting in evolutionary change. It is important in maintaining the adaptability of a species within a changing environment.

Summary

Human impact on biodiversity

Biodiversity describes the variety of living organisms on a local, national or global scale. **Global biodiversity** consists of approximately 2 million identified species of organisms in the **biosphere** (living world), and there are many more yet to be discovered. Over 50% of all known species are insects and most of these are species of beetle. When asked what could be inferred about the work of the Creator from a study of his works, the British biologist J. B. S. Haldane is reported to have replied 'an inordinate fondness for beetles'. Global biodiversity is influenced greatly by global warming (see A2 Unit 1). The emphasis in this chapter, however, is **local biodiversity** — the variety of life in Northern Ireland.

Threats to local biodiversity

Northern Ireland has lost over 50 species in the past century. Threats to biodiversity include habitat loss and fragmentation, including loss of native woodland, pesticide use and the establishment of invasive species.

Habitat loss and fragmentation

Knowledge check 52

How may the digging of drainage ditches have had a detrimental effect on habitats?

Knowledge check 53

Explain how the use of fertilisers has led to a loss of biodiversity.

Knowledge check 54

What is habitat fragmentation and why is it detrimental?

Habitats have been lost as a result of a number of activities relating to **intensive agricultural practices**, such as drainage schemes, removal of trees and hedges, and nutrient enrichment of soils. **Drainage schemes** were introduced to increase the area of agricultural land. As a result, many **wetland habitats** (e.g. rush pastures, raised bog, fens, reedbeds and wet woodlands) have been lost and these habitats are among the most important for wildlife — lapwing (*Vanellus vanellus*) numbers decreased by over 60% in the period 1987–99. The **removal of trees and hedgerows**, again to allow for more intensive agricultural practices, has also meant habitat loss for a variety of birds and other wildlife. The **nutrient enrichment of soils**, through the increased use of chemical fertilisers (containing the ions required by plants), has seen **species-rich hay meadows** decline by over 90% during the past 50 years. Many native grasses and herbs have become adapted to surviving in nutrient-poor soils (e.g. common bent grass, *Agrostis capillaris*, lady's bedstraw, *Gallium verum*, and the greater butterfly-orchid, *Platanthera chlorantha*). However, with the application of fertilisers, agriculturally preferred species of grass (e.g. perennial rye-grass, *Lolium perenne*) are able to grow much more quickly and out-compete the native plants. Anything that has a negative influence on plants has a similar effect on animal species. For example, one of the native plants in decline is devil's-bit scabious (*Succisa pratensis*), which is the main food plant for the caterpillars of the marsh fritillary (*Euphydryas aurinia*), a butterfly similarly in decline.

Where areas of habitat are lost, fragmentation of small pockets of habitat can result. This means that some species become isolated as small separate populations within these pockets. This leads subsequently to inbreeding within the isolated populations and a loss of genetic diversity, leaving species less able to adapt to changes in their environment and ultimately increasing the risk of extinction. The previously extensive network of hedgerows acted as wildlife corridors for many species (e.g. small mammals, birds, reptiles, amphibians and insects), allowing dispersal and migration between habitats.

Loss of native woodland

The felling of trees for agricultural land, as fuel and as building material, occurred centuries ago. Northern Ireland is presently the least wooded region of Europe, with an approximate total tree cover of 6% (European average is 31%). Only 1% consists of mixed-species broadleaf semi-natural woodland (i.e. woodland which had some form of human modification in the past). The remaining 5% consists of introduced, exotic conifers (e.g. Sitka spruce, *Picea sitchensis* and lodgepole pine, *Pinus contorta*). Coniferous forests tend to have a thick floor of undecomposed needles, little light penetration and a soil that is acidic. As a result there are few plant species among the understory or ground layer. Since the trees have been introduced, few native animals are adapted to live there. Such conditions are not conducive to species biodiversity. There are, however, remnants of native forest — for example Banagher Glen Nature Reserve in County Londonderry, which contains mostly sessile oak (*Quercus petraea*), and Breen Wood Nature Reserve in County Antrim, which is dominated by sessile oak, but with some pedunculate oak (*Q. robur*), an understory of rowan (*Sorbus aucuparia*), hawthorn (*Crataegus monogyna*), holly (*Ilex aquifolium*) and hazel (*Corylus avellana*), and a ground layer with varieties of ferns, grasses and other flowering plants. These patches of woodland display enormous biodiversity. You can get an appreciation of this diversity by visiting the website www.virtualvisit-northernireland.com, following the links 'see and do', 'nature and wildlife', then select 'Banagher Glen'.

Pesticides

Intensive agriculture was developed to maximise crop yield per unit area of land. It involved the creation of large open fields to make it easier to use mechanised machinery, and this also necessitated hedgerow removal. A single crop species is grown, which requires the addition of artificial fertilisers to maximise yields. As a **monoculture** (growing a single species), the crop plants are vulnerable to disease and pest problems, necessitating the application of chemical **pesticides**. Pesticides include **herbicides** (toxic to plants other than the crop), **fungicides** (toxic to fungi, e.g. cereal mildews) and **insecticides** (toxic to insects). The introduction of pesticides is associated with a huge loss in biodiversity — some farmland birds have declined by over 80%. There are several reasons:

- Pesticides may affect the soil ecosystem adversely by killing soil organisms. This will also adversely impact on other species in the food web.
- Pesticides may become ineffective and their long-term use may even result in an increase in pest numbers. This is because:
  - pesticide resistance will occur if the pest species evolves
  - pest resurgence — pesticides may remove the natural enemies (e.g. predator) of the pest species, so allowing the pest to return in even greater numbers
  - secondary pest outbreak will occur if a minor pest, previously kept at low numbers, multiplies rapidly in the absence of its competitor
- Herbicides reduce plant species diversity (with the removal of weed species in fields and in hedgerows if the spray drifts there). Therefore, the food available to many animal species in the food web is reduced, resulting in a lower diversity of animal species.

Invasive species

'Non-native invasive species' are species from other countries that establish themselves successfully in our habitats. They damage the 'native species' by out-competing them for habitat or food, preying on them, altering their habitat and by introducing disease and parasites. Invasive species usually do not have natural predators to control their numbers. For example, grey squirrels (*Sciurus carolinensis*), which are native to North America, threaten red squirrels (*S. vulgaris*) and woodland. They out-compete the red for food and are a known vector for the parapox virus that can be fatal to red squirrels. Grey squirrels cause economic loss to forest plantations by stripping the bark of young trees, which can lead to tree death.

Two species of flatworm, the New Zealand flatworm (*Artioposthia triangulata*) and the Australian flatworm (*Australoplana sanguinea var. alba*) have been introduced into Ireland. Both species predate earthworms and have significantly reduced earthworm numbers in some areas. This has had a hugely negative impact: earthworms are responsible for aerating the soil, decomposing plant material and are a food source for many animals, for example the song thrush, *Turdus philomelos*.

Knowledge check 55

State how Simpson's index (*D*) for a mixed woodland of native trees compares with that for a conifer plantation.

Knowledge check 56

Why might the use of pesticides be ineffective in controlling the numbers of pest species?

Examiner tip

The pesticide warfarin, which has been used to control rat populations, is less effective in many parts of Britain as rat populations have evolved resistance.

Rhododendrons are much admired garden plants, but *Rhododendron ponticum* is an invasive shrub that out-competes native species for resources, particularly light.

More information on invasive species can be found at www.invasivespeciesireland.com. After habitat destruction, invasive species are the second greatest threat to biodiversity worldwide.

Strategies used locally to encourage biodiversity

Woodland management

It is planned to increase tree cover in Northern Ireland from the present 6% and, in particular, to increase the cover by native trees. (A list of some native trees is provided in Table 9.) It is to be accomplished in a number of ways:

- encouraging farmers to plant native species, in hedges and field margins or in less fertile farmland
- restoring existing natural and semi-natural broadleaf woodlands
- establishing new plantations of native species — for example oak and ash, which will allow the growth of an understory of smaller trees, such as hawthorn and rowan, which in turn will provide conditions for many species of ferns and flowering plants in the herb layer.

Native species provide a habitat and food for a large variety of insects and other invertebrates (see Table 9).

Table 9 The number of species of insects associated with Irish trees

Tree species	Tree type	Associated insect species
Oak (*Quercus* spp.)	Native, deciduous	284
Willow (*Salix* spp)	Native, deciduous	266
Birch (*Betula* spp.)	Native, deciduous	229
Hawthorn (*C. monogyna*)	Native, deciduous	149
Blackthorn (*Prunus spinosa*)	Native, deciduous	109
Scots pine (*Pinus sylvestris*)	Native, conifer	91
Ash (*Fraxinus excelsior*)	Native, deciduous	41
Spruce (*Picea* spp.)	Non-native, conifer	37
Sycamore (*Acer pseudoplatanus*)	Non-native, deciduous	15

Woodlands of native species support a more complex community and will have a massive effect on increasing biodiversity in Northern Ireland. This is not to say that conifers do not support biodiversity — for example, the red squirrel and the long-eared owl show a preference for coniferous woodland.

Hedge restoration and management

Farmers are encouraged to plant new hedges and replant hedges that have become gappy through neglect. A mixture of species must be planted (as a double row) and hedgerow trees must be included. The aim is to include a range of species and so provide a variety of niches for a large diversity of animal species.

Knowledge check 57

What aspects of biodiversity should be considered in any biodiversity action plan?

Good hedgerow management through trimming also aims to promote biodiversity. The basic principles of good trimming are as follows:

- maintain a variety of hedge heights and widths to provide the optimum range of habitats (different bird species have particular preferences with respect to hedge height and width)
- trim in January or February to avoid destruction of birds' nests (March to August) and allow the berry crop to be used by wintering birds (September to December)
- trim on a 2- or 3-year rotation rather than annually, to boost the berry crop and insect populations
- avoid trimming all hedges in the same year (to allow hedge diversity)
- avoid cutting hedgerow trees (assuming they are native species)

Knowledge check 58

Why is the annual cutting of hedgerows detrimental to biodiversity?

Sustainable agricultural practices

There are trends now in agriculture to move away from monoculture, extensive applications of artificial fertilisers and ill-considered use of pesticides.

A traditional method was to grow different crops in one field over successive years — crop rotation. Crop rotation can improve soil fertility as different crops make different demands on soil nutrients. It can also help to avoid the development of diseases that are specific to only one crop. Polyculture is also being used. In polyculture crops are planted with a view to their mutual benefit. For example, a crop that attracts a natural predator of aphids helps a nearby crop that is infested with aphids. The need for pesticides is therefore eradicated.

The use of artificial fertilisers is now more judicious. Soils are tested for the level of different nutrients (i.e. ions) and fertiliser applied according to specific needs. There is also an increased use of organic fertiliser. This aids soil structure as well as releasing nutrients over time as it decomposes.

Broad-spectrum pesticides kill a wide variety of species and damage ecosystems:
- by killing the natural enemies of the pest
- by killing soil organisms
- by harming aquatic ecosystems through drift and run-off into waterways

Narrow-spectrum pesticides are toxic to a few species and so can be used more specifically to target the pest species.

It is important that a particular pesticide does not enter the food chain. For example, warfarin is a rodenticide used to kill rats that can damage grain stores. However, it has also been responsible for killing barn owls (*Tyto alba*). Now, new rodenticides are used that can be used in lower concentrations and are not harmful to barn owls.

Areas of farmland left undisturbed

Some farmers have **set-aside land**, which is never grazed or cultivated, to provide a habitat for a wide variety of species. They are also encouraged to leave an **ungrazed margin of grassland** at field perimeters. The aim is to provide additional habitat and food sources for a range of insects, birds and mammals. This strategy should contribute to the recovery of priority species such as linnet, yellowhammer, tree sparrow, barn owl and bats. It is also thought that these strips of land will provide a habitat for natural predators, for example some beetles, and so encourage pest control. For this reason, such margins are called **predator strips**. There is also support for farmers to plant native trees within the field margins. These strips extend the wildlife corridors along which many species can move between habitats.

Species-specific action

Each species has its own adaptations to its ecological niche. Therefore, there are specific considerations to be made with respect to individual species. There is a particular **action plan** for each threatened species, prepared nationally and at local council level. These detail the special considerations for improving numbers of the species in question. For example, some ground-nesting birds (e.g. the corncrake, *Crex crex*, now disappeared from Northern Ireland) have been affected detrimentally by the change from cutting grass towards the end of summer (to make hay) to making several cuts through the year (to make silage). Other species have been affected adversely by the switch from spring planting of cereal crops to autumn planting, a practice that means ploughing takes place in the autumn and there is no winter stubble left with remnant grain for seed-eating birds. This has had a negative impact on yellowhammers (*Emberiza citrinella*) and tree sparrows (*Passer montanus*). The ground also has plant cover in the spring, which reduces nesting sites for skylarks (*Alauda arvensis*).

Habitat and species protection

Designating special areas for protection is an effective way of conserving the biodiversity of Northern Ireland. Different designations are shown in Table 10.

Table 10 Designations of sites for the protection of habitats and wildlife

Designation	Description
Areas of Special Scientific Interest (ASSI)	These have been identified by ecological surveys as containing valued plant and animal species, and are managed with the cooperation of the landowners. There are over 200 ASSIs in Northern Ireland (e.g. Drumlisaleen).
Special Areas of Conservation (SAC)	These are given special protection under the EU Habitats Directive to help conserve some of the most seriously threatened habitats and species across Europe. There are 54 SACs in Northern Ireland (e.g. Peatlands Park).
Special Protection Areas (SPA)	These are given special protection under the European Commission on the Protection of Wild Birds (the Birds Directive) as important areas for breeding, over-wintering and migrating birds. There are 15 SPAs in Northern Ireland (e.g. Rathlin Island).

Designation	Description
Nature Reserves	These are areas of importance for plant and animal species and are directly managed for their conservation. There are almost 50 Nature Reserves in Northern Ireland (e.g. Banagher Glen Nature Reserve).
Marine Nature Reserve	The purpose of a Marine Nature Reserve is to conserve an exceptional range of marine organisms on the seashore and seabed. Northern Ireland has one Marine Nature Reserve, Strangford Lough.

Examiner tip

More information on protected areas is available on the website www.ni-environment.gov.uk/protected_areas_home.htm

Summary

- Habitats, and the organisms adapted to life there, have been lost as a result of activities relating to intensive agricultural practices, such as drainage, removal of trees and hedges, and nutrient enrichment of soils.

- Habitat loss can lead to fragmentation so that populations of particular species become isolated. The consequence of this is a loss of genetic diversity and adaptability.

- Native woodland represents a particularly rich habitat for a large number of species and its loss has greatly reduced biodiversity.

- The use of pesticides (herbicides, fungicides and insecticides) on farmland has caused a number of environmental problems. These include mobility into other habitats (aquatic and soil) with adverse effects there, toxicity to non-target organisms, pest resurgence, secondary pest outbreaks and the evolution of pest resistance.

- Non-native, invasive species represent a major threat to native species.

- Strategies that have been developed to encourage biodiversity include the planting of native trees, hedge restoration and management, and a variety of sustainable agricultural practices.

- Sustainable agricultural practices include a more judicious use of fertilisers, the use of crop rotation and a reduction in pesticide use with a move towards narrow-spectrum pesticides. There is also support for areas of farmland to be either left undisturbed or managed to encourage biodiversity.

- Locally, nationally and internationally, species action plans have been established for the conservation and management of certain threatened species.

- A number of habitats are being conserved and managed through the designation of special areas of protection.

Questions & Answers

This section consists of two exemplar papers constructed in the same way as your AS Unit 2 examination papers. Following each question, there are answers provided by two students of differing ability.

Examiner's comments

Each question is followed by a brief analysis of what to look out for when answering the question (shown by the icon ⓔ). All student responses are then followed by examiner's comments. These are preceded by the icon ⓔ. They provide the correct answers and indicate where difficulties for the student occurred. Difficulties may include lack of detail, lack of clarity, misconceptions, irrelevance, poor reading of questions and mistaken meanings of examination terms. The comments suggest areas for improvement.

Using this section

You could simply read this section, but it would be more effective to:

- try the questions before looking at the students' responses and/or the examiner's comments, allowing yourself 1 hour 30 minutes for each paper
- check your answers against the students' responses and the examiner's comments
- use the answers provided in the examiner's comments to mark your paper
- use the students' responses and the examiner's comments to check where your own performance might be improved

Tips for answering questions

Make sure that your answer is sufficiently detailed. The examiners give you guidance about how much you need to write.

- Use the mark allocation. In general, the number of marks indicates the number of points that you should provide — for a question worth 4 marks you need to make more points than for a question worth 2 marks.
- Use the recommended time allocation. You are advised to spend 20 minutes on Section B. Try to keep to this. It is possible to write a longer 'essay' but you may be providing more points than there are marks available.

Read the questions carefully. There are two aspects to this:

- Pay attention to the command terms used in each question — for example 'describe' or 'explain' — and make sure you respond appropriately.
- The stem of a question may provide information needed to answer the question. Think about how this information can help you to construct or focus on a relevant answer.

Exemplar paper 1

Section A

Question 1

If a blood vessel is broken (for example, following injury to the skin) thromboplastin is released and sets in motion a chain of reactions resulting in a blood clot.

(a) Complete the flow diagram below which summarises the clotting process.   (3 marks)

Sometimes the clotting process may be initiated in an unbroken blood vessel. An internal clot, known as a thrombus, is formed. The condition is known as a thrombosis.

(b) Explain the possible consequences of a thrombus.   (2 marks)

Total: 5 marks

ⓔ This is the type of question that you might expect early in an AS Unit 2 paper, targeted at the E-grade candidate. Part (a) tests recall of key steps in blood clotting — notice that you have to complete four names for 3 marks. In part (b), you must consider the consequence of a thrombus — notice that you are told that a thrombus is an *internal* clot.

Student A

(a) Thromboplastin ✗ → thrombin (✓) and fibrinogen ✓ → fibres ✗ **a**
(b) A thrombosis in the brain could cause a stroke ✓. **b**

ⓔ **2/5 marks awarded a** Thromboplastin is a clotting agent involved in the conversion of prothrombin to thrombin; fibrinogen converts to fibrin which forms the fibres of the clot. However, the technical term is required. Student A's two correct answers earn 1 mark. **b** This is correct, for 1 mark. To earn the second mark, some comment should have been made about either 'a thrombus causing a blockage' or the consequence of 'tissue not receiving oxygen'.

Student B

(a) Prothrombin ✓ → thrombin ✓ and fibrinogen ✓ → fibrin ✓

(b) A thrombosis reduces blood flow and if it happened in a coronary artery the cardiac muscle would be deprived of oxygen ✓ and the person would suffer a cardiac infarction ✓.

e **5/5 marks awarded a** This response is rewarded with full marks (i.e. 3 marks) for four correct answers. **b** This full answer with good use of the appropriate terminology scores both marks.

Question 2

The graphs below illustrate the effect of two different forms of selection (A and B) on the frequency of a characteristic within a population. In each case the upper graph represents the starting frequencies of the characteristic and the lower graph illustrates the outcome of the selection process.

(a) **Which of the two selection types, A or B, represents stabilising selection? Give a reason for your choice.** (2 marks)

(b) **Which of the two selection types, A or B, could result in a possible evolutionary change in the population? What is this type of selection known as?** (2 marks)

Total: 4 marks

ⓔ This is a straightforward question as long as you read the information carefully. Part (a) asks which form of selection represents stabilising selection. Even if you cannot recall the graphs that illustrate this, you should be able to work it out. In part (b), you are given crucial information when asked about evolutionary change — which outcome represents a change from the starting position?

Student A

(a) B ✗ — since the graphs are more or less the same shape ✗. a
(b) A ✗ — directional ✓ b

ⓔ **1/4 marks awarded** a It is graph A that represents stabilising selection. This is distinguished by a mode that remains the same, and where the extreme variants have been eliminated. The student fails to score. b It is graph B that shows a shift in the characteristic in the population. It is directional selection that leads to evolutionary change, for 1 mark.

Student B

(a) A is stabilising selection ✓ because a non-changing environment maintains the frequency of a desirable trait ✗. **a**

(b) B ✓ and directional selection brings about evolutionary change ✓ **b**

ⓔ **3/4 marks awarded a** The choice of A is correct, for 1 mark. However, the reasoning is not sound. Stabilising selection might be expected in a non-changing environment but that is not the evidence here — the mode is the same and extreme forms have been removed. **b** B is correct and this is directional selection, for 2 marks.

Question 3

Sand dunes may differ in their species composition. The diagram below is a vertical section through one particular sand dune system.

Describe how you would sample the area depicted in the diagram and use the results to illustrate quantitatively the zonation of the vegetation.

(6 marks)

Total: 6 marks

@ This question assesses AO3 — understanding of biology as an experimental science. In this case, you are asked about how you would undertake an ecological study of an area where there is obvious zonation. Notice that 6 marks are available, so a detailed answer is required.

Student A

Set a line transect through the dunes ✓ and place quadrats ✓ along this at 5 metre intervals ✓. Calculate the total percentage cover of all the plants in the quadrat ✗. Then put the results in a table and compare the different percentage covers of different zones within the sand dunes ✗.

@ **3/6 marks awarded** There are only three correct points given here. It is not sufficient to determine the total percentage cover of all plants — the determination must be for each species. No attempt is made to suggest how the zonation would be illustrated — for example by a series of kite diagrams (one for each species) with percentage cover (*y*-axis) plotted against position along the sand dunes.

Student B

You would start at the embryo dunes and randomly sample ✓ the area using quadrats ✓. You would determine the percentage cover ✓ of each plant species. You would then move to the next area and continue ✓ until the landward area is reached. You would record the results.

@ **4/6 marks awarded** Student B has provided the basis of a sampling procedure: random sampling; sampling at sites transecting the dunes; use of quadrats; determination of percentage cover to measure abundance. However, there is no reference to the identification of plant species — for example using a key — and no attempt to suggest how the zonation would be illustrated — for example by a series of kite diagrams (one for each species) with percentage cover (*y*-axis) plotted against position along the sand dunes. The question is not answered fully. Student B needs to pay more attention when reading the question.

Question 4

The diagram below shows a section through an alveolus and associated structures.

Squamous epithelium

Septal cell

Alveolar air space

Monocyte

Capillary endothelium

(a) The septal cell shown in the diagram above secretes surfactant. **What is the role of surfactant in the alveolus?**

(1 mark)

(b) State one adaptation, shown in the diagram, which facilitates gaseous exchange. Explain how this adaptation aids gaseous exchange.

(2 marks)

(c) State one adaptation, *not* shown in the diagram, which is needed for efficient gaseous exchange. Explain how this adaptation aids gaseous exchange.

(2 marks)

(d) State a role for the monocyte shown in the diagram.

(1 mark)

Total: 6 marks

ⓔ Parts (b) and (c) ask you to recall adaptations for gaseous exchange. This seems straightforward, but you need to be careful since (b) asks for one *shown* in the diagram while (c) asks about an adaptation *not shown* in the diagram. Parts (a) and (d) ask about the role of cells within the alveoli that are not involved directly in gaseous exchange. This is a test of your understanding of biological terms.

Student A

(a) To reduce the surface tension ✓ a
(b) Thin membranes ✗. This results in a greater rate of diffusion ✗. b
(c) There are millions of alveoli making up the lungs ✓ and these greatly increase the surface area over which gas exchange can take place ✓. c
(d) To digest any worn out organelles ✗ d

☉ 3/6 marks awarded a This is sufficient to obtain the mark, though a fuller answer would note that a reduction in surface tension prevents the walls of the alveoli sticking together and collapsing during exhalation. **b** The term 'membrane' can be confusing. The student should have noted that the cells of the alveolar walls are thin — they form a squamous epithelium. The *rate* of diffusion is not altered — it is the distance over which the gases have to diffuse that is reduced. The important thing to remember here is to be precise. The student fails to score. **c** The diagram does not show the vast number of alveoli, so this is correct, as is the explanation. The student earns 2 marks. **d** It is lysosomes within cells that 'digest worn-out organelles'. Monocytes develop into macrophages that ingest any bacteria present. The student fails to score.

> ### Student B
>
> **(a)** Surfactant reduces the surface tension preventing the polar water molecules on the inner walls of the alveoli from sticking together ✓. **a**
> **(b)** The wall of the alveolus consists of a squamous epithelium in which the cells are thin ✓. This means that the diffusion distance is short ✓. **b**
> **(c)** A layer of moisture lines each alveolus ✓. Gases must dissolve in water before they can diffuse through the cells ✓. **c**
> **(d)** The monocyte moves into the alveolus where it becomes a macrophage that engulfs any bacteria ✓. **d**

☉ 6/6 marks awarded a This is correct, for 1 mark. **b** This correct answer earns both marks. **c** This is correct, for 2 marks. **d** This is an excellent answer, which is well worth the mark.

Question 5

The yellowhammer, *Emberiza citrinella*, is a member of the bunting family. It feeds on grain, weed seed and grass seed in winter, though in summer adults and chicks feed mainly on invertebrates.

(a) The table below shows the classification of *Emberiza citrinella*. Complete the table by inserting the names of the three missing taxonomic groups.   (2 marks)

Kingdom	Animalia
	Chordata
Class	Aves
	Passeriformes
Family	Emberizidae
	Emberiza
Species	*E. citrinella*

(b) In Northern Ireland the yellowhammer has declined by 65% over the past 30 years, and is the subject of a Northern Ireland Species Action Plan. Recommendations to reverse this decline include the following:
  - limit the use of herbicides
  - reduce the use of insecticides
  - restore areas of rough grass left undisturbed at field margins

Explain how each of these recommendations might aid the recovery of the yellowhammer population in Northern Ireland.   (3 marks)

(c) As we have so little native woodland in Northern Ireland, hedges are an important substitute for woodland edge habitat. As such they host a wide range of nesting birds. Different species of bird have different preferences with respect to the structure of the hedge, as shown in the table below.

Species	Preferred height of nesting site in hedge	Preferred hedge width (if any)
Yellowhammer	Low (< 1 metre)	Wide (> 2 metres)
Bullfinch	Very high (> 4 metres)	Wide
Chaffinch	High	
Goldfinch	High	Wide
Greenfinch	High	Wide
Linnet	Low (< 1 metre)	

Use this information to explain why it would be preferable to trim farmland hedges on a 3-yearly rotational basis, rather than annually.   (2 marks)

(d) Apart from providing nesting sites for birds, suggest two other benefits of hedges to the biodiversity of Northern Ireland.   (2 marks)

Total: 9 marks

ⓔ In part (a), notice that you need to provide three taxonomic groups for the 2 marks available. A simple mnemonic may help you to remember groups — KPCOFGS (see p. 43). In part (b), you are required to use the information supplied in the question, together with your understanding of biodiversity, to explain aspects of a Species Action Plan for the recovery of yellowhammer numbers. Part (c) asks you to evaluate information in the question and demonstrate understanding of hedgerow management, aspects of which are also tested in part (d).

Student A

(a) Phylum (✓), division ✗, genus ✓ **a**

(b) Yellowhammers eat weed seeds in the winter and these may be covered in herbicides which could poison the yellowhammers. Insecticides may also be toxic ✓. Areas of rough grass left undisturbed would be free of herbicides and insecticides ✗. **b**

(c) This would allow the hedges to grow upwards and outwards so providing birds with their preferred nesting sites ✓. Cutting annually may kill the hedges ✗. **c**

(d) Hedges provide shelter for cattle ✗. They provide safe pathways for animals to move without attracting the attention of predators ✓. **d**

ⓔ 4/9 marks awarded a Phylum and genus are correct, for 1 mark. Division is another name (mostly used within the plant kingdom) for a phylum. **b** 1 mark has been allowed for the possible toxic effect of pesticides (herbicides and insecticides). The student fails to use the information provided in the question stem: that the yellowhammer relies on weed seed (which herbicides would remove) during the winter, relies on insects (killed by insecticides) as food during the summer, while areas of undisturbed rough grass would represent a source of both seeds and insects throughout the year. **c** High, wide hedges are preferred by some species and so 1 mark is awarded. However, some bird species prefer low hedges. In essence, a 3-year rotational trimming regime should mean that, at any one time, some of the hedges (i.e. those recently cut) are low while some (those uncut) would be high and wide, i.e. there would be a variety of hedge types to suit different species. **d** The first answer, while a correct statement, does not provide a benefit to 'biodiversity' as asked for in the question. The second is correct and earns 1 mark.

Student B

(a) Phylum (✓), order ✓, genus ✓

(b) Herbicides kill weeds and so the yellowhammers would have no weed seeds to feed on in the winter ✓. Insecticides kill insects which yellowhammers feed on during summer ✓. Restoring areas of rough grassland provides a sanctuary for grass, weeds and insects which are important food sources for the yellowhammer ✓.

(c) Many species prefer high nesting sites and wide hedges and trimming the hedges every three years allows time for these to grow ✓. Short hedges do not suit four of the six species ✗.

(d) Many hedgerow plants produce berries that are food for a variety of animals ✓. They represent wildlife corridors that allow animals to move safely between areas ✓.

ⓔ 8/9 marks awarded a All are correct for 2 marks. **b** This excellent answer earns all 3 marks. **c** High, wide hedges are preferred by some species and so 1 mark is awarded. However, some species prefer low hedges. A 3-year rotational trimming regime can be planned to produce a variety of hedge types to suit all species. **d** This excellent response scores both marks.

Question 6

The photograph below is of part of a transverse section through the root of a buttercup (*Ranunculus*).

HERVE CONGE, ISM/SPL

Draw a block diagram to show the tissue layers in the root as shown in the photograph.
Label the drawing to identify at least four structures.

(8 marks)

Total: 8 marks

ⓔ This question assesses drawing skills and the ability to identify structures shown in a photomicrograph of a buttercup root. Study the photograph to identify the obvious tissue layers and then draw them with smooth, continuous and non-sketchy lines. You must draw the structures in the photograph provided —— *not* provide a textbook diagram of a root. The proportionality of structures must be reasonably accurate. There are 4 marks for drawing skills and 4 marks for identification.

Student A

Xylem ✓

Phloem ✓

Endothelium ✗

ⓔ **5/8 marks awarded a** This is a block diagram of the tissues obvious in the photograph ✓. It is also an attempt to represent the photograph ✓ though it lacks the proportionality of the features shown ✗ since the xylem region is too small within the stele. The lines drawn are smooth and continuous, and not sketchy ✓. The student gains 3 marks for drawing skills. **b** The labels for xylem and phloem are correct, for 2 marks. However, endothelium is not acceptable for endodermis. Other recognisable features include the stele (vascular cylinder) and the cortex.

Student B

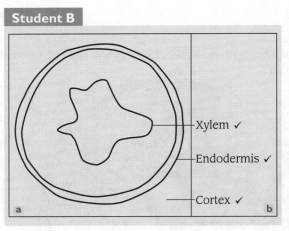

Xylem ✓

Endodermis ✓

Cortex ✓

a   b

ⓔ **5/8 marks awarded** **a** This is a block diagram showing only the xylem and endodermis tissue layers and so it lacks completeness ✗. It is an attempt to represent the photograph ✓, but it lacks the proportionality of the features shown ✗. The lines drawn are smooth and continuous, not sketchy ✓. The student gains 2 marks for drawing skills. **b** The student scores 3 marks for correctly labelling xylem, endodermis and cortex. The phloem is not drawn and so not recognised.

Question 7

Read the passage below and then use the information in the passage, and your own understanding, to answer the questions that follow.

The corncrake (*Crex crex*) is a small bird of the family Rallidae. It arrives in Ireland from mid-April, and the rasping call of the male, which is used to attract a mate, used to be one of the most familiar sounds of the summer. It no longer breeds in Northern Ireland. Secretive and difficult to see, corncrakes prefer to remain concealed in long grass, nettles and other tall vegetation. They feed on a range of invertebrates taken from plants or from the ground.

Nests are constructed on the ground from dead stems and leaves among the tall vegetation of hayfields and farm grassland. A first brood of ten eggs is produced in late May with peak hatching dates in mid-June. Females feed the chicks for the first few days and stay with them for about ten days. A second brood, again of ten eggs, is produced by the beginning of July with hatching taking place in late July.

A hundred years ago the population was measured in the tens of thousands. By the late 1960s the population had declined to less than 10 000. Since then, all-Ireland censuses have been carried out by recording the number of 'singing' males. In 1988, only 916 singing males were heard; in 1993 the number of singing males had fallen to 174.

These declines correspond to the replacement of traditional farming systems by modern agricultural methods. Increasingly sophisticated machinery meant that grass could be cut earlier in the year and the harvest was completed more quickly than previously. Farmers also began to take several crops of grass per year. Earlier mowing destroys nests and kills chicks which are reluctant to leave the cover of tall grass, and may become trapped in an island of remaining grass at the centre of the field if mowing proceeds from the outside of the field inwards.

At present, corncrakes only breed in isolated pockets in the west of Ireland — for example on the islands off the coast of Donegal. By late September the surviving birds migrate to Africa where they overwinter before returning in the following spring.

(a) **Describe the ecological niche of the corncrake.** (2 marks)

(b) **The survival rate of chicks, prior to migrating to Africa, is 40% when reared in traditional hayfields, while the survival rate of adult birds from their migration in the autumn until their return in the following spring is 25%. Use this information to explain why corncrakes must raise two broods annually to be successful.** (2 marks)

(c) **Using the information in the passage about the numbers of calling males, calculate the percentage decline of corncrakes in Ireland in the 5-year period 1988 to 1993. (Show your working).** (2 marks)

(d) **Suggest one reason for using 'the number of singing males' to estimate the numbers of corncrakes, and one reason why this method might not be valid.** (2 marks)

(e) **A number of schemes have been designed to develop favourable conditions for the improvement in corncrake numbers. Suggest two strategies that would be beneficial to corncrakes.** (2 marks)

(f) **With a small and fragmented population of corncrakes in Ireland there is a danger of inbreeding, which would result in a loss of genetic diversity. Explain why genetic diversity (variability) is important to populations.** (2 marks)

Total: 12 marks

(e) You must read the information in the passage on the ecology of the corncrake very carefully. You may benefit from highlighting key points. Part (a) asks about the ecological niche of the corncrake. If you understand the term 'niche', then the information is supplied in the passage. In part (b), you need to use both the information in the passage (i.e. ten eggs in each brood) and within the question stem to provide an appropriate answer, which should be supported by calculations. Part (c) requires a calculation of percentage decline — this is calculated as the difference divided by the earlier figure (in this case the numbers in 1988). Even if your calculation is incorrect, if you show your working you could be awarded marks for correct method. Part (d) looks at the validity of using 'singing males' to estimate corncrake numbers. Part (e) requires you to apply your understanding of biodiversity schemes. Part (f) changes tack, testing you on the general importance of genetic diversity.

Student A

(a) It nests in fields of tall vegetation ✓. a

(b) As most young corncrakes are wiped out during migration, a second brood must be raised so there are enough to maintain the population ✗. b

(c) 916 − 174 = 742 ✓ c

(d) The birds are hard to see and so the males that sing can be heard and recorded easily ✓. Because there could be more females than males, not a 1:1 sex ratio, which would mean that there are more corncrakes than estimated ✓. d

(e) Farmers might only take one crop of grass a year. The grass could be cut later in the year when the chicks have left the nest ✓. e

(f) Genetic differences allow the species to be more adaptable ✓. f

(e) 6/12 marks awarded a The student describes an important aspect of the corncrake's habitat, but fails to expand on what it is doing there — feeding on invertebrates as a secondary consumer. The student scores 1 mark. b This answer does not use the relevant data to support the conclusion and the student fails to score. See Student B's answer for a fuller response. c The question asks for the percentage decline. The student only gives the decline (1 mark) and should have divided this by the starting number (i.e. 916) to obtain a percentage (81%). d These suggestions are well thought out and worthy of both marks. e These answers are not distinct, i.e. the second answer depends on the first. The second sentence scores 1 mark. See Student B's response for a fuller answer. f This is sufficient for 1 mark. For the second mark reference should be made to how genetic diversity might allow a species to survive an environmental change and be capable of evolving.

(a) The corncrake lives in long grass, nettles and other tall vegetation ✓. It feeds on a range of invertebrates taken from plants or the ground ✓, and it constructs nests on the ground. a

(b) Because there is a chick survival rate of 40%, if only one brood was raised only four chicks would survive ✓. Then, if only 25% of the birds survive migration and return next spring this would only leave one bird. So two broods means that two birds will survive ✓, thus maintaining population numbers. b

(c) 916 (in 1988) less 174 (in 1993) = 742 ✓; 742 ÷ 916 × 100 = 81% ✓ c

(d) This is because males sing to attract a mate. Counting these shows the number of males capable of reproducing ✗. d

(e) Harvest the grass later in the year when both broods have hatched ✓ and promote set-aside grassland suitably managed ✓. e

(f) If there were an outbreak of disease, genetic diversity would prevent all of the population from being wiped out ✓. f

🅮 **9/12 marks awarded** a This excellent answer earns both marks. b This answer demonstrates a good understanding of the situation and explains it well (although reference could have been made to the need for two surviving birds to balance any adult losses). The student scores both marks. c This answer is correct, for 2 marks. d This is not really to the point. The reason for relying on the number of singing males is that the birds are so difficult to see. The problem with this is that it is not possible to know if all calling males are breeding (i.e. have been successful in attracting a mate) or if they attract and mate with one or more females. The student fails to score. e Both of these are suitable suggestions, for 2 marks. f This is sufficient for 1 mark. For a second mark, reference should be made to the possibility of *resistant forms* occurring within the variation shown.

Question 8

The graph below shows pressure changes that take place in the left side of the heart during one complete cardiac cycle.

Legend:
- – – Aorta
- —— Ventricle
- ···· Atrium

(a) At what time does the atrioventricular valve close? Give the reason for your answer. (2 marks)

(b) At what time does the aortic valve close? Give the reason for your answer. (2 marks)

(c) Explain the changes in the atrial pressure from 0.1 to 0.45 seconds. (2 marks)

(d) Explain the increase in the aortic pressure between 0.16 and 0.3 seconds. (2 marks)

(e) The pressure in the right ventricle reaches a maximum of 3.5 kPa. Give reasons for the difference between this pressure and the maximum pressure achieved in the left ventricle, as shown in the graph. (2 marks)

Total: 10 marks

ℯ Study the pressure changes carefully before you attempt to answer the questions. To answer (a) and (b) correctly, you must *work out* from the curves what changes in blood pressure cause the valves to close. To answer (c) and (d) well, you must apply your understanding of the cardiac

CCEA AS Biology

cycle to *explain* the changes in pressure. Part (e) might seem straightforward, but you must think carefully about the structure of the left and right ventricles and about where blood is pumped from each.

Student A

(a) 0.1 s ✓. This is when the atrium contracts, forcing blood into the ventricle and therefore increasing its pressure ✗. a

(b) 0.4 s ✓. This is when the aortic pressure is at its highest, so the valve closes to prevent backflow ✗. b

(c) Between 0.1 s and 0.12 s the atrium is contracting and pumping blood into the ventricle ✗. Thereafter, between 0.2 s and 0.45 s blood is returning to the atrium ✓. c

(d) Pressure increases as blood is forced into the aorta from the ventricle where the pressure is higher ✓. d

(e) This is because the wall of the left ventricle contains more muscle ✓. This is required to produce a higher pressure to pump the blood around the whole body ✓. e

🅔 **6/10 marks awarded** a The time is correct, for 1 mark. However, the reason given is irrelevant. The ventricle is contracting at this time, but even this is not the precise answer. At this time, the pressure in the ventricle increases to become greater than that in the atrium, so forcing the atrioventricular valve closed. b Again, the time is correct, for 1 mark, but the reason given is not. Most particularly, a valve does *not* close to prevent backflow. In this case, it closes because the pressure in the ventricle drops below that in the aorta. As a result, backflow is prevented. c The first part of this answer is incorrect. The second is correct, for 1 mark. The atrium contracted prior to 0.1 s. The peak in atrial pressure between 0.1 s and 0.14 s is due to the rise in ventricular pressure forcing the valve flaps to bulge into the atrial space (prior to blood forcing the aortic valve open). d This is correct for 1 mark, though a more complete answer would have noted that the semilunar value at the base of the aorta has been forced open. e Both parts are correct. An alternative answer would be to note that a low pulmonary pressure is required since slow blood flow increases the efficiency of gas exchange in the lungs, and also prevents fluid being forced into the alveoli. The student scores 2 marks.

Student B

(a) The atrioventricular valve closes at 0.1 s ✓, as contraction of the ventricle causes its pressure to increase above that in the atrium ✓. a

(b) The aortic valve closes at 0.4 s ✓, as the ventricle relaxes and the ventricular pressure decreases and becomes less than that in the aorta ✓. b

(c) There is a peak at 0.14 s as initially ventricular pressure increases though blood cannot exit the aorta and so the pressure pushes the flaps of the closed atrioventricular valve so that they dome into the atrium ✓. From 0.2 s, the pressure in the atrium increases gradually because the atrium is passively filling with blood from the pulmonary vein ✓. c

(d) Since the ventricular pressure is greater than the aortic pressure ✓ the semilunar valve is forced open ✓ and blood is pumped into the aorta increasing pressure there. d

(e) The muscular wall of the left ventricle is much thicker to pump blood into the aorta ✓. e

🄮 **9/10 marks awarded a** Both the time and reasoning are correct. The student scores both marks. **b** Student B has a good understanding of the operation of the heart valves and scores both marks. **c** Both statements are correct and indicate sound understanding. The student scores both marks. **d** Both marks are gained. **e** This is correct for 1 mark, but no reference is made with respect to the *reason* for the higher pressure generated — see Student A's response and the examiner's comment.

🄮 **Section A total for Student A: 30 marks out of 60**

Section A total for Student B: 49 marks out of 60

Section B

Quality of written communication is awarded a maximum of 2 marks in this section.

Question 9

> **Give an account of the processes involved in the movement of water through a plant.** (13 marks)
>
> **Total: 15 marks**

ⓔ In answer to this question (worth 15 marks) you must write in continuous prose since 2 marks are available for quality of written communication (QWC). This is a big topic, so take some time to devise a plan. Be aware that 'the movement of water through a plant' involves what happens in the root, in the stem and in the leaf. You must be able to sequence your ideas and emphasise the links between cause and effect, which is how QWC will be assessed.

Student A

In the root, water travels from cell to cell via two routes: the symplast and the apoplast ✓. Apoplast is when the water travels through each cell ✗, whereas symplast is when water travels along the cell walls ✗. However, water cannot pass through the Casparian strip ✓ and so must enter the cell before passing into the xylem ✓. Water is then drawn upwards by negative tension, adhesion and cohesion. Negative tension is the force produced by water evaporating out of the leaves ✗. Adhesion is when the polar water molecules ✓ are attracted to the sides of the xylem ✓. Cohesion is when water molecules are attracted to each other ✓. Once the water travels up the stem it enters the leaves. The water is then passed from cell to cell and once it reaches the outer layer of cells next to the air space it evaporates ✓ and is released through the stomata. a QWC b

ⓔ **9/15 marks awarded** a Seven appropriate points are provided, so Student A scores 7 marks. Some statements are simply wrong — for example, the symplast and apoplast routes have been confused. Other statements are not sufficiently precise: water does not evaporate out of the leaf; water vapour diffuses out following evaporation from the mesophyll surface. A number of relevant points (for example reference to the endodermis in the root) have been omitted. You should read Student B's answer for a fuller response. b The student expresses ideas clearly, even though there are some factual errors, and the account is reasonably well sequenced. The student scores 2 marks for quality of written communication.

Student B

Water enters the root and moves through the cortex via the apoplast or symplast pathways ✓. Using the apoplast route, water moves through the cellulose cell walls ✓. This is the main route ✓ since there is less resistance to movement. Water moves through the cytoplasm of cells and from cell to cell via plasmodesmata ✓ using the symplast route ✓. Water can only move through the endodermis, and into the xylem, using the symplast route ✓.

Forces of adhesion between the water molecules and the lignified xylem vessels ✓ help the water to creep up the xylem ✓. The force of cohesion, due to the attraction between water molecules, maintains a continuous water column ✓. This water column moves up as water leaves the xylem to replace ✓ the water that has evaporated from the mesophyll surface ✓ and diffused out of the open stomata ✓. Throughout, water is moving along a water potential gradient ✓ as transpiration creates a particularly negative water potential in the leaf ✓. a **QWC** b

ⓔ **15/15 marks awarded** a The student receives a maximum 13 marks for the content. b This is a well-structured account and ideas are expressed fluently. The links within the overall process are made clearly. The student scores 2 marks for quality of written communication.

ⓔ **Overall, Student A scores 9 marks and Student B scores 15.**

Section B total for Student A: 9 marks out of 15

Section B total for Student B: 15 marks out of 15

ⓔ **Paper total for Student A: 39/75 marks (grade D).** The poor performances in the answers to the first two questions (targeted at the E-grade candidate) show that the student has not undertaken a full revision of the course. Answers to other questions (e.g. questions 3 and 4) are reasonable but lack the required detail. The student would benefit by ensuring that the number of points made in an answer equates to the mark value of the question part. There is also evidence that the student did not use information provided in question stems (e.g. in questions 5 and 7). The student did not always know the appropriate biological term (e.g. question 4(d)) and needs to work at numeracy skills (question 7). More thorough revision and greater practice at answering (and carefully reading) questions would undoubtedly improve the student's performance.

ⓔ **Paper total for Student B: 64/75 marks (grade A).** The student demonstrates thorough knowledge of topics across the course and the ability to use a wide range of biological terms appropriately. There are some areas for improvement (for example, drawing skills in question 6). The student also demonstrates a wide range of skills, including numeracy skills. The student is able to apply understanding so that data interpretation and the ability to analyse and evaluate information, including novel information, are well illustrated.

Exemplar paper 2

Section A

Question 1

Use the dichotomous key below to identify the five kingdoms of living organisms. In each case, name the appropriate kingdom.

(5 marks)

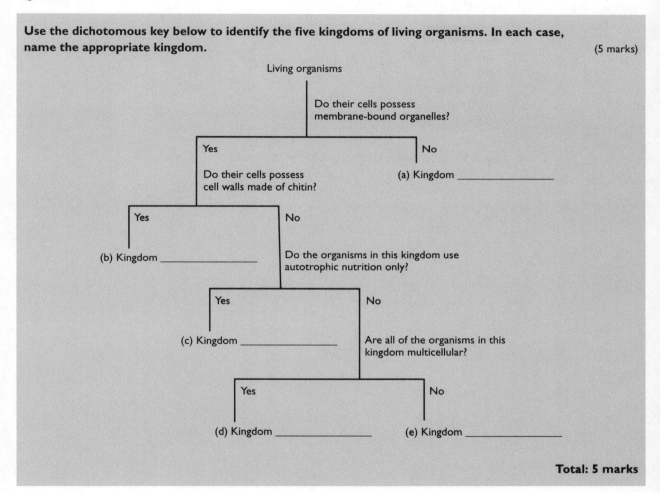

Total: 5 marks

ⓔ This is straightforward provided that you give careful consideration to the question asked at each step. You may benefit by listing the five kingdoms and then decide where each fits in the key. No kingdom can appear twice. You should go over your responses to check that you have not made any silly mistakes.

Student A

(a) Protoctista ✗
(b) Fungi ✓
(c) Plantae ✓
(d) Animalia ✓
(e) Prokaryotae ✗

ⓔ **3/5 marks awarded** The student has confused Protoctista with Prokaryotae. The other three kingdoms are correct, for 3 marks.

Student B

(a) Prokaryotae ✓
(b) Fungi ✓
(c) Plantae ✓
(d) Animalia ✓
(e) Protoctista ✓

ⓔ **5/5 marks awarded** Student B scores all 5 marks.

Question 2

The diagram below illustrates the structure of the leaf of a xerophyte.

- Outer epidermis
- Schlerenchyma fibres
- Vascular bundle
- Photosynthetic tissue

(a) (i) List two features, present in the diagram, which would operate to reduce transpiration. **(2 marks)**

   (ii) Explain how one of the above features operates to reduce transpirational water loss. **(2 marks)**

(b) Identify two features of the leaf of a hydrophyte, and explain how each acts as an adaptation to environmental conditions. **(2 marks)**

Total: 6 marks

ⓔ In (a)(i), you must identify two xerophytic features *shown in the diagram* — do not refer to something that is not illustrated. In (a)(ii), an explanation of how one of the features reduces transpiration is required — you must be precise here since there is a tariff of 2 marks. Part (b) asks for two features of hydrophytes and also how each acts as an adaptation. In general, the question is testing your ability to offer full and accurate answers.

Student A

(a) **(i)** Leaf hairs ✓, rolled-up leaf ✓ **a**

   (ii) Leaf hairs trap humid air ✓ and reduce transpirational water loss ✗. **b**

(b) Large prominent air spaces provide buoyancy ✓, and stomata on the upper surface allow gas exchange with the atmosphere ✓. **c**

ⓔ **5/6 marks awarded** **a** Two correct features are given, for 2 marks. **b** The 'trapping' of humid air is correct for 1 mark. However, the consequence is not explained. The humid air outside the open stomata reduces the diffusion gradient for water vapour out of the leaf and so less is lost. **c** The student gives two features that are correct for hydrophytes, the second only just sufficient (see Student B's answer for a better, fuller response) and scores 2 marks.

(a) **(i)** The leaf is folded or rolled inwards ✓, large air spaces ✗ **a**
  (ii) The folded leaf causes an increase in humidity at the lower surface ✓ so reducing the diffusion gradient for water vapour out of the open stomata ✓. **b**
(b) The leaf possesses hairs that aid flotation ✗, and stomata on the upper surface to allow for gas exchange with the atmosphere, a much richer source of gases, particularly oxygen, than the water ✓. **c**

ⓔ **4/6 marks awarded a** The first feature is correct, for 1 mark. However, the second is not — large air spaces are a hydrophytic adaptation. **b** This excellent answer scores both marks. **c** The student shows some confusion between hydrophytic and xerophytic adaptations. However, the second feature is correct (and well explained), for 1 mark.

Question 3

(a) **The diagram below shows an artery and vein in part of the pulmonary circulation.**

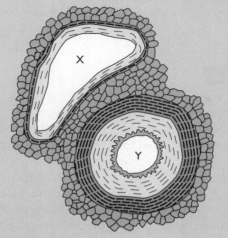

    (i) **Identify which of the two, X or Y, represents an artery.** (1 mark)

    (ii) **Describe two features of an artery and explain how each is adaptive in the functioning**
         of the artery. (2 marks)

    (iii) **Describe one feature of a vein and explain how it is adaptive in the functioning of the vein.** (1 mark)

(b) **Outline the sequence of events which result in the inhalation (inspiration) of air into the lungs.** (4 marks)

                                                     Total: 8 marks

🅮 In part (a), you are presented with a diagram that you are expected to use to show understanding of the functioning of arteries and veins. This is relatively straightforward, although in (ii) and (iii) your answers must explain how features are adaptive, i.e. give reasons as to how they are adaptive. Part (b) is simple recall on the events of inhalation — a full, well-sequenced answer is required.

(a) **(i)** Y ✓ a

     (ii) Elastic fibres to withstand high pressure and allow recoil ✓; collagen fibres for
            strength ✗ b

     (iii) Possesses pocket valves ✗ c

(b) During inhalation, the pressure in the lungs is lower than outside and so air
     rushes in ✓, causing the diaphragm to descend ✗. The external intercostal
     muscles contract, which pulls the rib cage upwards and outwards ✓. This
     increases the thoracic volume ✓, allowing the lungs to inflate. d

🅮 **5/8 marks awarded** a This is correct, for 1 mark. The artery has a thicker wall and a smaller lumen than a vein. b The first adaptation is correct. However the reference to collagen is not a specific adaptation in the functioning of the artery. The artery has a thick layer of smooth muscle which, when it contracts, reduces the blood flow to the organ that it supplies. The student scores 1 mark. **c** This is correct, but the student makes no attempt to explain why valves are adaptive — for example, that they ensure one-way flow towards the heart. The student fails to score. **d** There are three correct points here. However, there is confusion with respect to cause and effect within the inhalation process. The contraction of the diaphragm is a major cause of the increase in thoracic volume and in bringing about the inhalation of air — it does not result from inhalation. Student A scores 3 marks.

Student B

(a) (i) X ✗ a

(ii) Elastic fibres to allow for expansion and recoil ✓; possesses a small lumen ✗ **b**

(iii) They have a large lumen which ensures that there is little resistance to blood entering into and passing through the vein ✓. **c**

(b) The muscles of the diaphragm contract causing the diaphragm to move downwards ✓. The external intercostal muscles contract and the ribs are caused to move up and out ✓. This increases the volume of the thoracic cavity ✓. The pressure surrounding the lungs is therefore decreased ✓ with the result that air flows into the lungs along the pressure gradient. **d**

ⓔ **6/8 marks awarded a** This is incorrect, although from the answers below this seems like a slip. **b** There is no attempt to explain why having a small lumen is an adaptive feature — it ensures that high blood pressure is maintained. Student B scores only 1 mark. **c** This is well explained for 1 mark. **d** This full answer scores all 4 marks.

Question 4

The graph below shows the frequency distribution of birth weights of infants in a London hospital between 1935 and 1946 (histogram) and the infant death rate in relation to birth weight (broken line). (Weight is shown in Imperial units, pounds; the unit is represented by lb.)

(a) Describe the trends shown in the graph. (3 marks)

(b) The data in the graph are often presented as an example of stabilising selection. Explain what is meant by stabilising selection, and its influence on the weight of infants. (4 marks)

Total: 7 marks

ⓔ The graph illustrates stabilising selection and you are told this in the question. Your answers *must* relate to the information supplied. Before you attempt to describe trends in part (a), make sure that you understand fully the measurements on the axes. One relationship illustrates the births; the other shows infant death rate. In *describing* trends you should make conclusions about what is happening — not just quote values from the graph or note that a curve goes down and then goes up. Part (b) requires you to offer *explanations* for the trends by *applying your understanding* of stabilising selection.

Student A

(a) The closer the birth weight is to the mean, the fewer infant deaths there are ✓. a

(b) Stabilising selection is apparent here since infants born close to the mean weight are favoured ✓. Those born further away from the mean weight have a reduced chance of survival ✓. b

ⓔ **3/7 marks awarded** a The student has not been penalised for using mean (rather than mode) and earns the mark. However, there are other relevant points that could have been made. These are provided in Student B's answer. b Both these points are correct and Student A scores 2 of the 4 marks available.

Student B

(a) The modal birth weight is between 6.5 and 7 lbs ✓. The greatest survival is among infants with these birth weights ✓. The highest death rate is among those infants with a birth weight at the extremes, i.e. below 5 lbs and over 9 lbs ✓. a

(b) Stabilising selection occurs when individuals near the mode are favoured ✓ and extreme forms tend not to survive ✓. In this example, infants of 7 lbs have the greatest survival rate ✓, so the constancy of the characteristic is maintained and the modal birth weight will remain at approximately 7 lbs ✓. b

ⓔ **7/7 marks awarded** a This excellent description of trends scores all 3 marks. b This is an excellent answer, which scores the full 4 marks.

Question 5

(a) Explain what happens to the partial pressure of oxygen and carbon dioxide within the blood capillaries in the lungs and in actively respiring tissues, such as working muscle.   (2 marks)

(b) The graph below shows oxygen dissociation curves for haemoglobin at two different partial pressures of carbon dioxide (pCO_2), and for myoglobin. The partial pressures of oxygen (pO_2) in the lungs, in muscle during moderate exercise, and in muscle during strenuous exercise, are indicated.

(i)   Which of the curves, B or C, represents the dissociation curve for haemoglobin in the lungs and in respiring tissues?   (1 mark)

(ii) What term is used to describe the effect of higher pCO_2 on the oxygen curve for haemoglobin?   (1 mark)

(iii) Using your understanding of oxygen dissociation curves, and the information provided in the graph, explain why haemoglobin unloads oxygen to actively respiring tissues, such as working muscle.   (3 marks)

(iv) Using your understanding, and the information provided in the graph, explain the role of myoglobin in a muscle.   (2 marks)

(v)   Curve B is the normal dissociation curve for human haemoglobin. Where would the haemoglobin dissociation curve for a llama, a mammal found at high altitude, lie in relation to curve B? Explain your answer.   (1 mark)

Total: 10 marks

e This question tests understanding of this topic, rather than just recall. In part (a), you are asked about what happens to *both* pO_2 and pCO_2 in the lungs *and* in working muscle — you must cover all of this to earn the 2 marks available. Part (b) requires you to provide biological reasons. In (b)(iii) there are 3 marks available for *using the information in the graph* to provide a full explanation of what is happening to provide working muscle with oxygen. Watch out in (b)(v) — the mark is for giving the reason and not just for saying where the curve lies.

Student A

(a) In the lungs, the partial pressure of oxygen increases, while the partial pressure of carbon dioxide decreases ✗. In the tissues, the partial pressure of oxygen decreases since oxygen is being used in respiration, which also produces carbon dioxide and so the partial pressure of carbon dioxide increases ✓. **a**

(b) (i) B in the lungs, C in the tissues ✓ **b**
(ii) Lower affinity ✗ **c**
(iii) In the tissues, oxygen is used up and in such circumstances haemoglobin unloads its oxygen ✓. **d**
(iv) Myoglobin has a high affinity for oxygen and can take up oxygen more easily ✗. It enables aerobic respiration to continue for longer ✓. **e**
(v) The llama haemoglobin curve would lie to the left of curve B (✓). **f**

e **4/10 marks awarded a** The answer about the levels of oxygen and carbon dioxide in the lungs does not gain a mark because it is not an explanation of the changes. The changes in the tissues are explained correctly in terms of respiration. Student A scores 1 mark **b** These are both correct, for 1 mark. **c** This is incorrect — it is called the Bohr effect. **d** This is fine for 1 mark, but does not go far enough since there is no mention of the effects of an increase in pCO_2 on oxygen unloading. Part (a) is relevant here and the student has answered that pCO_2 increases in the tissues due to respiration. Remember that questions are often structured so that one part builds on another. This question part is worth 3 marks and a fuller answer than that provided is necessary. **e** The first part of the answer is wrong since it is describing what happens in the lungs, not, as required, in muscle. The second part is correct, for 1 mark. **f** This is correct, but no reasoning has been presented and so the student fails to score.

Student B

(a) In the lungs, pO_2 increases while pCO_2 decreases, since oxygen is diffusing out of, and carbon dioxide into, the alveoli according to the diffusion gradients ✓. In the tissues, pO_2 decreases as oxygen is being used in respiration in the tissues cells, while pCO_2 increases because carbon dioxide is produced ✓. **a**

(b) (i) B in the lungs, C in the tissues ✓ **b**
(ii) Bohr effect ✓ **c**
(iii) In respiring tissues, oxygen is used up and pO_2 is reduced to 3 kPa and, during strenuous exercise, this can become as low as 1 kPa ✓. At lower pO_2 haemoglobin cannot hold on to its oxygen and so it is unloaded ✓. Respiration produces carbon dioxide and so pCO_2 increases with the effect that haemoglobin releases even more oxygen ✓. **d**

(iv) Myoglobin binds with oxygen and only releases it at very low pO_2 ✓. It acts as an oxygen store ✓ in muscle and enables aerobic respiration to take place for longer. **e**

(v) The haemoglobin dissociation curve for the llama would lie to the right of curve B ✗ since it must have a higher affinity for oxygen if it is to pick up oxygen at the low partial pressures found at high altitude. **f**

ⓔ **9/10 marks awarded** **a** The student notes the changes and provides explanations as required by the question, for both marks. **b** These are both correct, for 1 mark. **c** This is correct, for 1 mark. **d** This excellent answer contains more than three correct points. Note that the student makes appropriate use of the data in the graph. Student B scores all 3 marks. **e** Another excellent answer scores both marks. **f** The reasoning is correct, but since the positioning of the curve is wrong the student fails to score. This seems like a slip and indicates the value of checking your answers.

Question 6

The diagram below shows a simple bubble potometer. The potometer is used to measure the rate of water uptake by a cut, leafy shoot.

(a) (i) Describe how the potometer, as shown in the diagram, would have been set up. **(3 marks)**

(ii) Describe how the potometer would be used to make several measurements of the rate of water uptake. **(2 marks)**

(b) State one major assumption that is made when using this apparatus to measure the transpirational loss of water. **(I mark)**

(c) In order to investigate the effect of light on the rate of transpiration the following two experiments were devised:
- **Experiment I: a bench lamp was placed near to the shoot**
- **Experiment 2: a black plastic bag was placed over the shoot**

The following results were obtained:
- **Experiment I: at time 0 the bubble was at 5mm, and readings taken thereafter, at 2 minute intervals, were 20, 35, 50, 65, 79 and 93mm**
- **Experiment 2: the initial reading was 17mm and subsequent readings of 21, 25, 29 and 33mm were taken at intervals of 3 minutes**

(i) Organise the results into an appropriate table. Your table should have a caption, suitable column headings, show units and include all the data in such a way as to make interpretation easy. **(4 marks)**

(ii) Explain, as far as possible, the results obtained. **(2 marks)**

(iii) Evaluate the validity of the experimental design in investigating the effect of light on the rate of transpiration. **(2 marks)**

Total: 14 marks

ⓔ This question tests AO3 and your understanding of a piece of apparatus (the potometer). In part (a), you are required to show understanding of how it is used, while the validity of its use in investigating transpiration is asked for in (b). You are provided with the results of an investigation using a potometer in part (c). In (c) (i), you are asked to demonstrate your ability to organise the data into an appropriate table. Notice that you are directed about what you should include. The

CCEA AS Biology

caption must not simply say 'A table of results'. In (c) (ii), you must *interpret* the results – use your understanding to offer reasons for the trends indicated – and, in (c) (iii), *evaluate* the methodology – for example, have all variables been appropriately controlled.

Student A

(a) (i) The potometer is set up under water ✓. The end of the shoot is also immersed and the last centimetre of stalk is cut under water ✓. Vaseline is smeared round the base of the shoot and at the stopper in order to ensure that it is airtight ✓. a

(ii) Measure the distance travelled by the air bubble ✓ and reset the air bubble by opening the water reservoir ✓. b

(b) The transpirational loss of water is equal to water uptake ✓. c

(c) (i) d

Time/minutes	Experiment 1 Distance on scale/mm	Experiment 2 Distance on scale/mm
0	5	17
1		
2	20	
3		21
4	35	
5		
6	50	25
7		
8	65	
9		29
10	79	
11		
12	93	33

(ii) With the bench lamp, there was more water uptake due to photosynthesis occurring ✗. When a black plastic bag was covering the plant, only respiration was occurring so little water was taken up ✗. e

(iii) As rate of water uptake equals rate of transpiration, the experiment is valid ✗. However, the minute intervals were not the same for both, making comparison more difficult ✗. f

e **8/14 marks awarded** a Three correct points are given, for 3 marks. b The student scores both marks. c This is correct, for 1 mark. d There is no caption ✗ describing the contents of the table, even though this is specifically asked for. The independent variable is in the first column, appropriately titled and with the unit of measurement shown ✓. Column headings for the dependent (measured) variable are not explanatory — the experiments could be about any topic ✗. Nevertheless, the table does have a logical construction, includes all the data and allows the data to be readily compared ✓. 2 marks are awarded for table construction. e In part (b), the student has established that this apparatus is essentially measuring transpiration, but ignores this here. References to photosynthesis and respiration do not explain the results. The student fails to score. f The first statement relates to the validity of using the apparatus (as answered in part (b)), and not to experimental design. Taking measurements at different times may mean that greater care is required when tabulating the results or plotting a graph, but it does not affect the validity. This is about there being more than one different variable in each experiment: the lamp provides heat as well as light; being covered by a black plastic bag means that, as well as light not being available, there are no air currents and so humidity increases. The student fails to score.

Student B

(a) (i) The shoot should be inserted into the potometer while it is fully immersed in water ✓. Vaseline may be used to create an airtight seal ✓. **a**

   (ii) The distance moved by the air bubble is measured over a fixed time (e.g. 10 minutes) ✓. The experiment is then repeated by opening the reservoir and re-setting the air bubble ✓. **b**

(b) That water lost by transpiration is replaced equally by water taken up ✓. **c**

(c) (i) Results for the potometer **d**

Potometer experiment with a benchlamp placed near the shoot		Potometer experiment with a black bag placed over the shoot	
Time/minutes	Distance moved by air bubble/mm	Time/minutes	Distance moved by air bubble/mm
0	0	0	0
2	15	3	4
4	30	6	8
6	45	9	12
8	60	12	16
10	74		
12	88		

   (ii) Placing the bench lamp near the shoot means that the stomata are open and water vapour may escape ✓. Covering the shoot with a bag increases the humidity inside and reduces the diffusion gradient so less water is lost by transpiration ✓. **e**

   (iii) The lamp should have been placed a fixed distance from the plant. All other variables (temperature ✓, humidity) should have remained constant. **f**

🅮 10/14 marks awarded **a** There are two correct points, for 2 marks. Other points could have been made — for example immersing the whole apparatus to remove any air. **b** The student scores both marks. **c** This is correct, for 1 mark. **d** A caption of 'Results for the potometer' is not nearly full enough ✗. An appropriate caption would be 'An investigation into the effect of light on the rate of transpiration using a potometer', since it includes the independent variable (light here) and explains what is being measured (transpiration here). The independent variable is in the first column (and the third) and with the unit of measurement shown ✓. The column headings for the dependent variable are fully explanatory and are shown as 'Distance moved by bubble' by zeroing the initial value and subtracting it from subsequent values which eases a comparison of the two sets of data ✓. Nevertheless the construction of table would have been more logical if the data had been presented against a single column of time intervals as in Student A's table ✗. 2 marks are awarded for table construction. Table construction is a skill to be practised – see the AS Unit 3 guide. **e** Both statements are correct. The student scores 2 marks. **f** This is correct for experiment 1, but the student offers no answer for experiment 2 and, therefore, scores only 1 mark – see the examiner's comments to Student A's answer.

Question 7

Most of the plantation forest in Ireland is conifer, mainly Sitka spruce (*Picea sitchensis*). A Sitka spruce forest was surveyed for nesting bird species. The numbers of birds of each of four species found are shown in the table below.

Nesting bird species	Number of individuals
Goldcrest (*Regulus regulus*)	8
Siskin (*Carduelis spinus*)	8
Sparrowhawk (*Accipiter nisus*)	2
Treecreeper (*Certhia familiaris*)	4

(a) Calculate the value for Simpson's diversity index (*D*) for nesting bird species in the survey of the Sitka spruce forest. The formula for *D* is:

$$D = \frac{\sum n_i(n_i - 1)}{N(N - 1)}$$

where n_i = the total number of organisms of each individual species
   N = the total number of organisms of all species
   (Show your working.)   (3 marks)

In a mixed forest of Sitka spruce and ash (*Fraxinus excelsior*) a survey of nesting bird species indicated that there were 18 species present giving a Simpson's Index (*D*) of 0.06.

(b) Use this information to explain the term 'species richness'.   (1 mark)

(c) Explain the difference between the values of Simpson's index (*D*) for the Sitka spruce forest and the mixed Sitka spruce/ash forest. Both forests were of comparable size.   (2 marks)

(d) What do the results suggest about the strategy for planting future forests?   (2 marks)

(e) Sitka spruce is an 'introduced species'. State two problems associated with introduced species. (2 marks)

Total: 10 marks

ⓔ You are given the formula to use in the calculation and told what the symbols n_i and *N* represent, so (a) is a matter of using the numbers correctly. Don't forget that even if your answer is wrong, you can gain marks if your working is correct. This is why you must *show* your working. Parts (b) and (c) test your understanding of measures of biodiversity. Remember, in (c), that a low value for *D* indicates high biodiversity. In part (d) you are asked to *suggest* — provide a plausible biological explanation — what the impact of the findings should be for future forestry plantings. Part (e) tests the breadth of your knowledge of 'introduced species'.

(a) $D = [8(8 - 1) + 2(2 - 1) + 8(8 - 1) + 4(4 - 1)]$ ✓ $\div 20(20 - 1)$ ✗ $= 126 \div 380 = 0.33$ ✓ a

(b) There are a lot of different species ✓. b

(c) The mixed woodland has a smaller value for Simpson's index (D) ✓. It is not possible to comment on the amount of diversity ✗. c

(d) Forests should be planted according to their commercial value ✗. d

(e) Out-competing native species ✓. e

ⓔ **5/10 marks awarded** a The numerator part of the calculation is correct. The student has made a mistake in totalling the numbers column, which should be 22, not 20. However, the subsequent part is not penalised, since the arithmetic operation is correct and this can be seen clearly as the working out is shown. The mistake was a slip that would have been found if the student had checked the arithmetic. Student A scores 2 marks. b This is correct, for 1 mark. c This is correct (and seems an easy mark given that D for the mixed woodland is given in the stem of the question as 0.06). A smaller value for D indicates greater diversity. The student scores 1 mark. d This might be a correct point of view, but it is not appropriate here. The question asks for a consideration of the results, i.e. the increased diversity of mixed woodland. The student fails to score. e This is correct for 1 mark. Other correct responses include: lack of natural predators and so a lack of control; lack of association with native species and so a threat to biodiversity; elimination of native species by, for example, predation; hybridisation with native species.

(a) $D = [8(8 - 1) + 2(2 - 1) + 8(8 - 1) + 4(4 - 1)]$ ✓ $\div 22(22 - 1)$ ✓ $= 0.27$ ✓ a

(b) This is the number of species in one area ✓. b

(c) The Sitka spruce forest has a lower species diversity than the mixed forest ✓. A greater number of plant species is present, so there is a greater variety of possible nesting sites and food available for different bird species ✓. c

(d) It is preferable to have forests planted with a mixture of tree species ✓. This would increase the number of available niches for a variety of animal species, especially native species ✓. d

(e) Few organisms can feed on them so the variety of organisms in the area is reduced ✓. New diseases are introduced so native species may be wiped out ✓. e

ⓔ **10/10 marks awarded** a This is correct, for all 3 marks. b This is correct, for 1 mark. c This full answer scores both marks. d This is an excellent answer. Both marks awarded. e There are two correct points here, for 2 marks.

Section A total for Student A: 33 marks out of 60

Section A total for Student B: 51 marks out of 60

Section B

Quality of written communication is awarded a maximum of 2 marks in this section.

Question 8

> **Give an account of the phases of diastole, atrial systole and ventricular systole during the cardiac cycle. The account should make reference to each of the following:**
> * **the waves of excitation**
> * **the pressure changes**
> * **the opening and closure of valves**
>
> (13 marks)
>
> **Total: 15 marks**

ⓔ This is quite an involved essay and a plan will help you. As you describe the events of the phases of the cardiac cycle — diastole, atrial systole and ventricular systole — you must refer in each case to the wave of excitation over the cardiac muscle, the contraction (and relaxation) of atria and ventricles, the changes in pressure within the heart chambers and associated arteries and how pressure differences cause opening and closing of artioventricular and semilunar valves and the subsequent movement of blood. Do you see the benefit of a plan?

Student A

Diastole: This phase of the cardiac cycle is the resting phase. On the right side of the heart blood flows into the right atrium and on the left side it flows into the left atrium ✗. **a**

Atrial systole: During atrial systole the right atrium fills with blood from the venae cavae and the left atrium from the pulmonary veins ✗. The atria contract and increase pressure in the atria forcing blood into the ventricles ✓, since when the pressure in the atria is greater than in the ventricles the atrioventricular valves open ✓. Atrial systole begins with electrical activity being produced at the sinoatrial node ✓. **b**

Ventricular systole: During ventricular systole, the tricuspid and bicuspid valves are forced shut ✓ and prevent backflow into the atria. The semilunar valves are forced open ✓. This allows oxygenated blood from the left ventricle to enter the aorta, from where it will supply the organs of the body; blood from the right ventricle enters the pulmonary artery and is taken to the lungs ✓. The semilunar valves slam shut and the pocket-like valves prevent backflow to the ventricles ✗. **c QWC d**

ⓔ **7/15 marks awarded a** There is nothing incorrect here, it just lacks the detail necessary to earn a mark. For example, where is the blood flowing from (the major veins), what happens to the pressure in the atria, what effect has this on the atrioventricular valves? The student fails to score. **b** The atria fill with blood during diastole, not during atrial systole, and so the first statement is wrong. The second statement is correct. The opening of the atrioventricular valves actually occurs during diastole, but the concept is correct and so the third statement is awarded a mark. Then, there is a correct reference to the SA node initiating the wave of excitation. Student A scores 3 marks. **c** The student notes correctly that the atrioventricular valves are forced shut, and that, at a later time, the semilunar valves are forced open. However, there is no reference to the increasing pressure in the ventricles, that the atrioventricular valves are only forced shut when the pressure is greater than that in the atria and that the semilunar valves are forced open when the pressure in the ventricles is greater than in the major arteries. Semilunar valves close during diastole, when the pressure in the ventricles becomes lower than in the major arteries. Overall, while there is good understanding of the structure of the heart, there is a lack of understanding of the pressure changes and the electrical activity that coordinates the contractions. The student scores 3 marks here, giving a total of 6 marks for the biological content of this answer. **d** The ideas are not well sequenced, so the student scores only 1 mark for quality of written communication.

Student B

Diastole: During diastole the heart is relaxed ✗. **a**

Atrial systole: During atrial systole an electrical impulse is generated within the sinoatrial node ✓. This wave of excitation propagates over the walls of the atria and causes contraction ✓. This results in the remaining blood within the atria being pushed into the ventricles ✓. Blood flows down the pressure gradient and the atrioventricular valves are pushed open. **b**

Ventricular systole: The wave of excitation reaches the atrioventricular node ✓. The electrical impulses then spread downwards through the bundle of His ✓ and the Purkinje fibres, stimulating contraction of both ventricles from the apex upwards and pushing blood towards the arteries ✓. As the pressure in the ventricles increases, the atrioventricular valves are slammed shut ✓. As the pressure increases further it becomes greater than in the arteries and the semilunar valves are forced open ✓. **c**

Diastole: When the atria are relaxed blood is returned via the venae cavae (right atrium) and the pulmonary veins (left atrium) ✓. As blood returns, pressure increases and, when the ventricles relax, pressure in the atria increases to a point above that in the ventricles so that the atrioventricular valves are pushed open ✓. Both ventricles then fill passively ✓. **d QWC e**

(e) **13/15 marks awarded a** This is not sufficient for a mark here. However, some events of diastole are discussed appropriately later in the answer. **b** There are three correct points here, for 3 marks, although some detail is missing. The AV valves are already open during atrial systole, since the atrial pressure increases when blood is returned to the heart. **c** This is a reasonable account of ventricular systole though, again, some detail is missing — for example, there is no mention of the role of the chordae tendinae is preventing the AV valves turning inside out. Student B scores 5 marks. **d** Overall, this is a good account even if some detail has been omitted. Student B earns 3 marks here giving a total of 11 marks for the biological content of the answer. **e** This is a well-structured account and ideas are expressed fluently. The links between electrical activity and contraction, and between pressure changes and valve action, are made clearly. The student scores 2 marks for the quality of written communication.

Section B total for Student A: 7 marks out of 15

Section B total for Student B: 13 marks out of 15

ⓔ **Paper total for Student A: 40/75 marks (grade D)** This is a rather patchy performance and illustrates a lack of thorough preparation for the exam paper. Further, some answers do not respond to the command term used in the question, as in question 3 part (a) where explanations were required. Thorough revision and careful practice of examination questions will always bring their reward.

Paper total for Student B: 64/75 marks (grade A) The student shows both knowledge from across a wide range of topics and the ability to apply understanding, even in unfamiliar contexts. There is a high level of competence in analysing and evaluating information presented in a variety of forms. The overall impression is of a student of considerable ability who has prepared well for the exam.

1 Nitrate (and sulfate) ions.

2 Surface area = 22, volume = 6, so the surface area-to-volume ratio is 22:6 or 11:3.

3 Humans are terrestrial (with an impermeable body surface); they are large (small surface area-to-volume ratio); they have a high metabolic rate (large demand for oxygen).

4 They are especially small and have a biconcave disc (flattened) shape.

5 Diffusion

6 A good transport system has a pump (or equivalent), vessels and a fluid to transport materials around the body. It also has exchange surfaces to load substances into the transport system and to remove them where required.

7 It increases the surface area-to-volume ratio (more oxygen is absorbed relative to the amount required) *and* means that all tissues are close to the absorbing surface.

8 Plants lack muscle tissue, i.e. they do not move from place to place.

9 Leaves have an air-space system; they are thin (and broad); they have stomata that connect to the atmosphere.

10 They allow air to enter from the atmosphere: carbon dioxide for photosynthesis; and oxygen, which may diffuse down to the roots through an extensive air-space system, for respiration. Both oxygen and carbon dioxide are more plentiful in air than dissolved in water.

11 Ventilation of the lungs replenishes oxygen-rich air in the alveoli, thus increasing the oxygen diffusion gradient into the blood. It also replaces air that has a high carbon dioxide concentration with air that has a low carbon dioxide concentration, thus increasing the carbon dioxide diffusion gradient out of the blood.

12 Inhalation depends to the contraction of muscles of the diaphragm and the external intercostal muscles of the ribcage, while exhalation normally involves only the relaxation of these muscles.

13 The alveoli collapse and are difficult to expand, making breathing difficult and reducing the efficiency of gas exchange. Blood oxygen levels fall and carbon dioxide levels increase.

14 Emphysema reduces the efficiency of breathing (reduced recoil of alveoli due to loss of elasticity) and gas exchange (reduced surface area of alveoli). The overall result is that oxygen uptake is reduced greatly, so that less is available for the production of ATP in respiration — hence the difficulty in undertaking strenuous activity.

15 (a) Xylem is the star-shaped tissue located centrally in the root and on the inner sides of the vascular bundles in the stem.
     (b) Phloem is found between the arms of the xylem in the root and on the outer sides of the vascular bundles in the stem.

16 Xylem vessels lack cross walls, lack any cytoplasm (to impede the flow of water), are lignified (to keep them open and prevent them collapsing) and have pores (to allow water to leave laterally).

17 Companion cells contain numerous mitochondria that produce the ATP used to carry out active processes such as loading sucrose etc. into the sieve tubes.

18 Lack of oxygen would reduce the rate of aerobic respiration, which produces the ATP used in the active uptake of ions.

19 Root pressure results from the active secretion of ions into the xylem. A respiratory poison prevents the production of ATP used in active transport.

20 Water vapour diffusing out of the stomata is trapped and the region immediately outside becomes saturated. The water potential gradient between the inside of the leaf and the outside is reduced.

21 Very young leaves are removing sucrose from the phloem (they are a 'sink') while mature leaves are releasing sucrose since they are photosynthesising at a high rate (they are a 'source').

22 Substances enter the blood at the exchange (absorptive) surface. These substances have to be transported quickly enough to satisfy the organism's requirements (which will be great if it is large and active). Diffusion alone is not rapid enough.

23 A double circulation allows a two-pressure system with higher pressure to the body cells and lower to the lungs. High pressure in the systemic (body) circulation ensures that oxygenated blood is pumped efficiently to the body cells and allows the formation of tissue fluid. Low pressure in the pulmonary (lung) circulation ensures that fluid is not forced out into the alveoli and the slower flow of blood allows more time for gaseous exchange.

24 Vena cava, right atrium, right ventricle, pulmonary artery, capillaries in a lung, pulmonary vein, left atrium, left ventricle, aorta.

25 They have the same thickness of muscle and contract with equal force, since they only have to pump blood into the ventricles below.

26 The SAN initiates the heart beat by emitting impulses over the atria; the AVN delays these impulses and relays them to the bundle of His, which conducts it to the base of the ventricles.

27 (a) The delay allows time for the atria to empty before the ventricles contract.
     (b) By contracting from the base upwards, each ventricle forces all the blood towards the arteries.

28 They close when the pressure in the ventricles is greater than the pressure in the atria.

29 They are closed during diastole and atrial systole when the ventricle muscle is relaxed. They are also closed during the initial part of ventricular systole when the ventricle muscle contracts without raising the ventricular pressure above that in the artery. They are closed as long as the atrial pressure exceeds that in the ventricles.

30 60 s divided by 0.8 s = 75 beats min^{-1}.

31 Aorta, since the aortic pressure is much greater than that in the pulmonary artery.

32 They pick up oxygen in the lungs and release it in respiring tissues.

33 It has no nucleus, so has more room for haemoglobin (each red blood cell contains 250 million haemoglobin molecules). It is small and flattened, so has a large surface area-to-volume ratio. Being thin means that oxygen does not have to diffuse far to reach a haemoglobin molecule.

34 Polymorphs and monocytes (which develop into macrophages). Polymorphs are short-lived, while monocytes are long-lived.

35 Sucrose is transported in plants; glucose is transported in animals.

36 Thromboplastin (thrombokinase) converts prothrombin (a blood protein) to thrombin (another enzyme) which converts fibrinogen (another blood protein) to fibrin (which forms the fibres of the clot).

37 There are two factors — actively respiring tissues consume more oxygen and release more carbon dioxide. Both a decrease in pO_2 and an increase in pCO_2 cause more oxygen to be released from the haemoglobin.

38 At the pO_2 found in the placenta, fetal haemoglobin must be able to pick up oxygen when the maternal haemoglobin is releasing oxygen.

39 Test whether they can interbreed successfully and produce fertile offspring.

40 The Latin names are used internationally and are understood by scientists worldwide whereas common names can differ locally let alone internationally.

41 Plants are autotrophic (photosynthetic) containing chloroplasts with chlorophyll, while fungi are heterotrophic (lysotrophic); plants are multicellular, while fungi may be unicellular, but most are multicellular; plants store carbohydrate as starch, while fungi store carbohydrate as glycogen; plants have a cellulose cell wall, while fungi have one made of chitin.

42 (a) Chitin cell wall/cells organised into hyphae
(b) Animal cells never have a cell wall; they store lipids as fats

43 Both are heterotrophic and store carbohydrate as glycogen.

44 Because different species are both adapted and distributed differently in their environment.

45 Seed banks maintain a source of genetic diversity for crop plants. They contain genes that could confer subtle variations such as resistance to drought, frost or pests (which modern plants may lack, having been selected for increased yield).

46 A feature (behavioural, physiological etc.) that helps an organism 'fit' into its habitat, breed and pass on its alleles.

47 Edaphic factors are environmental factors that relate to the soil.

48 The rough periwinkle lives on the upper shore which is often left exposed so that released eggs would dry out; the smooth periwinkle lives in the middle shore which is frequently covered by water and tidal movements disperse the developing larvae.

49 (a) Sexually reproducing organisms — crossing over and independent assortment of chromosomes (during meiosis), and cross-fertilisation of gametes (as well as mutation).
(b) Asexually reproducing organisms — mutation only.

50 The loss of genetic diversity means that there are fewer different forms on which selection may act. There is less likely to be an individual with the relevant advantageous feature should the environment change.

51 Among the vast numbers of bacteria, a few may have natural resistance to penicillin. These are selected for, in that they survive and reproduce, passing on the allele for resistance. Therefore, the frequency of those with resistance increases in the population.

52 It may mean the loss of wetlands and all the species adapted to living there. There would be a reduction in biodiversity.

53 It leads to nutrient enrichment of the soil, which selects rapid-growth grass species. These outcompete plant species that are adapted to nutrient-poor soils and so results in a loss of biodiversity.

54 It means that a particular habitat, for example deciduous woodland, in split up into small pockets so that populations are isolated and prevented from interbreeding. This leads to inbreeding and a loss of genetic diversity.

55 Simpson's diversity index, D, would be lower for the mixed woodland than for the conifer plantation.

56 This is because of pesticide resistance, pest resurgence and secondary pest outbreak.

57 Species diversity, genetic diversity within species, ecosystem diversity

58 Only a few species are adapted to a habitat of short, well-trimmed hedges. A variety of hedge heights and thicknesses, resulting from a 3-year rotation of hedge trimming, will favour a greater biodiversity since some species will be adapted to conditions in tall, wide hedges while others will be adapted to short, narrow hedges.

59 A change in agricultural practice towards the cutting of grass crops several times a year to make silage.

60 Because to protect any individual species (such as an orchid) it is necessary to protect its habitat; and, more importantly, it is likely to be the whole community of plants and animals in the habitat that needs protection.

Note: key terms have **bold** page numbers.

CCEA AS Biology